WHAT
UKRAINIAN ELECTIONS
TAUGHT ME
ABOUT DEMOCRACY

Footprints Series

Jane Errington, Editor

The life stories of individual women and men who were participants in interesting events help nuance larger historical narratives, at times reinforcing those narratives, at other times contradicting them. The Footprints series introduces extraordinary Canadians, past and present, who have led fascinating and important lives at home and throughout the world.

The series includes primarily original manuscripts but may consider the English-language translation of works that have already appeared in another language. The editor of the series welcomes inquiries from authors. If you are in the process of completing a manuscript that you think might fit into the series, please contact her, care of McGill-Queen's University Press, 1010 Sherbrooke Street West, Suite 1720, Montreal, QC, H3A 2R7.

WHAT UKRAINIAN ELECTIONS TAUGHT ME ABOUT DEMOCRACY

JANE COOPER

McGill-Queen's University Press

MONTREAL & KINGSTON · LONDON · CHICAGO

ISBN 978-0-2280-2255-8 (paper)
ISBN 978-0-2280-2256-5 (ePDF)
ISBN 978-0-2280-2257-2 (ePUB)

Legal deposit third quarter 2024
Bibliothèque nationale du Québec

Printed in Canada on acid-free paper that is 100% ancient forest free
(100% post-consumer recycled), processed chlorine free

We acknowledge the support of the Canada Council for the Arts.
Nous remercions le Conseil des arts du Canada de son soutien.

McGill-Queen's University Press in Montreal is on land which long served
as a site of meeting and exchange amongst Indigenous Peoples, including the
Haudenosaunee and Anishinabeg nations. In Kingston it is situated on the
territory of the Haudenosaunee and Anishinaabek. We acknowledge and thank
the diverse Indigenous Peoples whose footsteps have marked these territories
on which peoples of the world now gather.

Library and Archives Canada Cataloguing in Publication

Title: What Ukrainian elections taught me about democracy / Jane Cooper.
Names: Cooper, Jane (Jane C.), author.
Series: Footprints series (Montréal, Quebec) ; 30.
Description: Series statement: Footprints series ; 30 | Includes bibliographical
    references and index.
Identifiers: Canadiana (print) 20240338499 | Canadiana (ebook) 20240338588 |
    ISBN 9780228022558 (paper) | ISBN 9780228022572 (ePUB) |
    ISBN 9780228022565 (ePDF)
Subjects: LCSH: Local elections—Ukraine—Kropyvnyts′kyï. | LCSH: Election
    monitoring—Ukraine—Kropyvnyts′kyï. | LCSH: Election workers—
    Ukraine—Kropyvnyts′kyï. | LCSH: Elections—Corrupt practices—Ukraine—
    Kropyvnyts′kyï—Prevention. | LCSH: Democracy—Ukraine—Kropyvnyts′kyï.
Classification: LCC JS6118.9.K76 C66 2024 | DDC 324.9477/6—dc23

CONTENTS

Preface

I didn't set out to accumulate records from my election missions to produce a book. However, when I went looking for sources for this project, I realized I had a large eclectic collection of personal materials, including detailed appointment diaries, letters, emails, photographs, scrapbooks, maps, music CDs, and far too much souvenir swag given out by foreign political parties, not to mention drafts of reports I had prepared on various assignments. Secondary sources included official reports published by the Organization for Security and Cooperation in Europe/Office for Democratic Institutions and Human Rights (OSCE/ODIHR) and other election observers, books, academic and gray literature along with contemporary news reports, and YouTube videos and Facebook posts (remarkably, many still online eight years after the events in 2015). And of course, we live in a world where you can revisit many of the streets you walked along years ago through Google Maps and Google Street View.

That said, any dialogue in quotation marks is at best an approximate rendering of what people said to me based on what I recorded in reports or letters soon after the conversation. Very few of the people I met in these stories spoke to me in English, so much of what I report was conveyed to me through an interpreter. What I heard may not have been quite what they said. And what I thought they meant may have been something quite different from what they wanted to convey. One of the challenges inherent in international observation is that you may have misunderstood what the people you met wanted to tell you. You can only do your best to try to understand. You ask multiple questions. You check your understanding with your partner and interpreter soon after the conversation. But a completely accurate rendering of what they said and meant remains elusive.

For many characters in this book, only first names have been used or names have been changed in the interests of privacy. However, what occurred in Kirovohrad in 2015, and the personalities involved, is a matter of public record.

Map of the places I observed elections in Ukraine: Odesa, 2002; Kharkiv, 2009–10; Dnipropetrovsk, 2012; Ivano Frankivsk, 2014; and Kirovohrad, 2015. Map provided by the European Commission's Emergency Response Coordination Centre.

Prologue

Kyiv, Ukraine, 22 November 2015

I am already in my ninth-floor hotel room when I get the phone call, half-undressed and getting ready for a shower. I look out the window over the glittering lights of the capital of Ukraine as I struggle to understand the rapid-fire Russian. The woman at the other end is distraught.

"I'm calling from poll 867. You have to come," she says. "They've changed half the commission members. They are going to eliminate all the ballots from our poll!" As I hear the agitated voices in the background, I can picture the woman – bundled up in her hand-knit toque and quilted winter jacket, phone pressed to her ear – surrounded by people on the steps of a school in the regional centre we had left the day before.

"I can't come," I have to tell her. "I'm already in Kyiv."

"But you have to see this!" I have seen the majority of the sixteen members of poll 867's polling commission fighting an uphill battle since the election the week before to get the results of their poll registered as they had counted them. They have been subject to a barrage of pressure from members of the District Election Commission, representatives of political parties, lawyers, judges, and reporters. But up to this night they have stood firm. They know there were no irregularities in the voting at their poll, and they know they had counted correctly. They ran a clean election. But it sounds like someone is about to pull the rug out from under their feet.

"I'm so sorry! We're not there anymore." I attempt to explain in my broken Russian that our international election observation mission is coming to an end, and the observers from around the country have all been called back to the capital.

Finally, she seems to grasp what I am saying. "Well, there's nothing you can do then!" she says and ends the call.

I sit down on the edge of the bed, deflated. This is probably the most disappointing moment I've had in my many years observing international elections. An honest local election official facing a blatant exercise to illegally remove votes from the count desperately wants the support of neutral international observers. She wants the whole sorry debacle fully on the record. But we can't complete that job. However, it isn't such a surprise. The story of how she and I got to this point is a telling tale of the strengths and the limitations of international election observation missions that I have come to understand over more than twenty-five years on the ground.

It is also a tale of the challenge of maintaining honest democratic processes when voters are so evenly divided that election winners and losers are separated by a tiny margin. This story is set in a small city at the centre of Ukraine, but it echoes political challenges faced across that country and in countries around the world.

I don't think I am a romantic. I'm not going to tell you that Ukraine is any more special than any other place on earth. Ukraine is as full of nuance and contradiction as any other country and Ukrainian politics are particularly so. But as we are challenged to stand by Ukraine as it faces war with Russia, we ought to learn something about the recent history and the real lives of the Ukrainian people.

WHAT
UKRAINIAN ELECTIONS
TAUGHT ME
ABOUT DEMOCRACY

Introduction

I

I was born curious. I always knew there was a much bigger world beyond my own backyard. This is why I have spent almost half of my forty-year career working in international development, which has brought the privilege of traveling all over the world and living for years at a time in southern Africa, South Asia, central Asia, and eastern Europe. And yet, however much I travel, I never tire of exploring both the differences and similarities encountered in each new country. You have never seen it all. There is always more to learn.

So, although I fell into international election observation more or less by accident, I was immediately drawn in by a mandate that drops you into a new place and then permits you to ask almost anybody almost anything. Whatever topic piques your interest, it is probably part of the wider context of the electoral contest you have been assigned to observe. And with your laminated credentials hanging around your neck on an official lanyard, and your pen poised over your notebook, most people are happy to tell you all about their experiences. There are few better assignments out there for a traveller with an insatiable curiosity.

II

Elections are important events. Casting a ballot during an election may be a simple action that many of us do with little thought. Unless your vote is subverted or taken away, it can be easy to forget how fundamental that process is to produce a government that has legitimacy in the eyes of the people. However, in many countries, trust that your vote will help choose the government that rules you is not a given.

A modern democracy is always at its core a feat of the imagination, relying as it does on faith and confidence in processes that are inevitably out of sight of the average citizen's eye. Voters have to believe that their vote matters, that it will be counted correctly, and that their voice will somehow be heard. Otherwise they will not come out to the polls.

An election observer has a license to peek behind the scenes to see how democracy can and does work. They also get to see how democracy can fail. A nuanced understanding of those failures is valuable because it can help us imagine something better. Revealing injustice is critical to defining a more just society. Despite what they taught us in university, democracy has little to do with the ancient Greek model where elite men in togas debated in a forum (without the participation of women, enslaved people, and anyone else who was not a citizen). Election observation takes you past the arcane theory and into the muddy reality of practice, to a place where we can learn about how we might make democracy better. As Francis Fukuyama points out, modern liberal democracy is a constant work in progress that waxes and wanes, but it keeps coming back because we find "the alternatives are so bad."[1]

As 2023 drew to a close, many experts agreed that democratic practices were waning in many countries around the world. International think tanks counted sixteen consecutive years where democratic freedoms had declined in more countries than had improved.[2] Others suggested that by 2022, up to thirty years of democratic advances had effectively been eliminated.[3] Pundits observed that democratic processes were increasingly undermined by uncompetitive elections, voter suppression, opaque election financing, the spread of misinformation, attacks on the media and civil society organizations, and the growth of autocratic governments and dictatorships.

When citizens lose confidence in democratic processes, much like a loss of confidence in a banking system, we risk a "run on democracy." However, in contrast to the long lines at the bank door that are the hallmark of a loss of confidence in financial institutions, a run on democracy is more likely to manifest in shrinking lines at the polls, as voters increasingly decline to turn up to cast what they see as a wasted ballot. That is a worrying trend evident in even the most established democracies like Canada, particularly at the municipal level. A mere 36 per cent of Ontario voters turned out for local elections in the fall of 2022.[4]

I learned a lot about the strengths and weaknesses of democracy from assignments as an international election observer with the Organization for Security and Cooperation in Europe (OSCE). I started in the central Asian republics of Tajikistan, Kyrgyzstan, and Kazakhstan, but the place I returned to most often was Ukraine. So, while I draw on my experiences in all the countries I have observed in for this book, the primary focus is Ukraine. I use examples from each election I observed to illustrate how democracy may, or may not, work. But the heart of this story is how I saw trust in democratic processes set back in one municipal election in 2015 in the central Ukrainian city of Kirovohrad. It is a lesson we all can learn from.

III

With the collapse of the Soviet Union, Ukraine became an independent republic in 1991. In a radical departure from seventy years of one-party rule, the new government was chosen through open multi-party elections. Independent Ukraine has since developed a vibrant political landscape, and many parties have emerged, merged, split, and dissipated over thirty years of independence. These political parties rarely have strong ideologies, and more often are political projects set up to back individual personalities with strong regional or ethnic identities. But voters do have plenty of choices.

Voters also usually have a long list of candidates to choose from for president. The president holds a powerful position, appointing the cabinet and the prime minister, which keeps him – and it has always been a man to date – at the centre of the political spotlight. Citizen activism in Ukrainian politics has a strong history, with mass demonstrations playing a major role in two out of five presidential transitions since independence. In 2004, during what came to be called the Orange Revolution, protesters forced a rerun of a flawed presidential election, effectively rejecting the purported winner of the presidency. Ten years later, during the Revolution of Dignity in 2014, also known as the Euromaidan movement, demonstrators overthrew the sitting president after he stepped back from government policy promoting integration with Europe.

Parliamentary politics are also lively. Half the members of the national legislative assembly – known as the Rada – are elected through proportional representation (PR) with parties needing 5 per cent of the national vote to be allocated Rada seats. The other half of the members of Parliament represent single-member constituencies. Given this combination of PR and single-member seats, small parties and independent members of Parliament can play an outsized role in the final composition of the government. Maintaining a government coalition in the Rada has been a constant battle, and periods of legislative gridlock have occurred. Debates in Parliament may stray far from policy and videos of unseemly brawls on the floor of the Rada have garnered thousands of views on YouTube.

Local government mirrors the national system, with the mayors and councillors in smaller cities and villages directly elected while the councils in larger municipalities are elected by PR from party lists. The PR system creates a very different political environment than we see in local politics in Canada, where party politics are frequently absent. Leading candidates for Ukrainian local government often run in multiple races. They may put their name on the list for mayor at the same time as they head a party list for district or city council. They may hedge their bets further with a simultaneous candidacy on the party list for regional council. Some may even already hold a seat in Parliament.

When voting in local elections is over, inevitably there is a round of intra- and inter-party jockeying for power. Local power brokers negotiate backroom deals over which candidates will actually take the seats on district, city, and regional councils, who may give up seats they hold elsewhere, and how their parties will put together the coalitions necessary to pass legislation in bodies splintered among multiple small parties. The voters have no role in this post-election horse-trading, and so have little idea when they cast their ballots who may eventually represent them. It is an opaque system that does little to build voter confidence and trust.

The OSCE has been invited to observe every major presidential, parliamentary, and local election in Ukraine since 1998. Accumulated OSCE reports show a rollercoaster cycle of electoral improvements and backsliding. Generally, Ukrainian elections have been praised for having a strong competitive environment, but the playing field has not always been level, with incumbents often exploiting their home ice advantage. Allegations of fraud are common, although proof can be hard to come by. The most consistent criticism has been biased reporting in the media, with business interests influencing how candidates are covered. On the other hand, the most significant improvement over the years has been the implementation of a regularly updated national voter registry. First used for the 2010 presidential election, the national registry replaced locally generated voters lists that had often been the source of fraud. Canadians can be proud that, alongside the US and the European Union, our government was a major contributor that helped the Ukrainian government build this registry.[5]

IV

Over the years observing elections internationally with the OSCE and in Canada, I have come to the conclusion that there are five basic approaches to triumphing in any election. Or, to look at it from the flip side, there are five key points when election interference has the potential to subvert the electoral process. This book is organized around my observations of how, over the course of an election, political actors do one or more of five things: prepare the field, win the votes, buy the votes, steal the votes, and/or invalidate the votes.

PREPARE THE FIELD

In many real-world elections, a winning field may be prepared far in advance by making it difficult or impossible for some candidates to run and/or preventing some voters from participating.

WIN THE VOTES
In the ideal world of free and fair elections, the successful party wins the votes by building a relevant platform, nominating credible candidates, and running a compelling campaign.

BUY THE VOTES
The balance may be tipped in the run-up to an election by secretly, or publicly, buying votes with gifts that influence the voter's choice

STEAL THE VOTES
On election day or during the ballot count, there is an endless list of ways that votes can be stolen.

INVALIDATE THE VOTES
After an election, losing parties may go to the courts to try to cancel or invalidate some or all of the votes cast against them.

Election observation involves looking for all five of these practices at all three levels of election administration – national, district,[6] and local – to put together an accurate picture of what is going on during an election. One of the roles of the short-term observers, who come in for a week to ten days around election day, is to monitor whether any vote stealing is going on at the polls or during district tabulation. Long-term observers who are in-country more than a month before the vote and at least a week after the election have more opportunities to understand the campaign, look for advance vote buying, and monitor whether votes are being invalidated after the election at the local and district levels. Members of a core team of observers working at the national level for two to three months are best placed to compile a national overview from the short-term and long-term observations; they report on all five options, from whether an uneven playing field has been prepared through to the validation of the final results.

In this book, I follow the story of how these five stages unfolded during local elections in 2015 in the Ukrainian city of Kirovohrad. Along the way, I have interspersed stories from other elections that I have observed that help illustrate the many ways these five generic approaches play out in practice. In fact, all five techniques can be seen in almost all elections. However, it is important to recognize that evidence of election interference – such as vote buying and vote stealing – does not always mean that the final result does not represent the will of the people. But whether or not meddling or manipulation changes the results, anything other than legitimately winning the votes erodes people's trust in the electoral process and constitutes a significant threat to democracy.

1   It's Not Over until It's Over

I

"Do you want to hear a joke about our local elections?" Gene asked with a grin. Local elections had just concluded across Ukraine that March of 2002. A stalwart member of our Odesa English Club, Gene came to the club to practice his language skills every Friday. He had graduated as a veterinarian but aspired to be a filmmaker, and I had come to appreciate his wry sense of humour.

"It goes like this: the assistant comes to the mayor the morning after the election with good news and bad news. 'The good news is you get to keep your job! The bad news is you still didn't get any votes ...'"

I laughed. The Black Sea port of Odesa had a reputation as the humour capital of Ukraine, so jokes about local politics were to be expected. But like all really funny jokes, this one was rooted in reality.

That spring of 2002, I was on a ten-month assignment as a civil society adviser with a Canadian non-governmental organization (NGO) project in the Black Sea port city of Odesa. A couple of days earlier, over fries at McDonald's, I had asked some younger English Club members who they would vote for in the upcoming local elections. Half of them declared they had no intention of voting. The other half thought they might vote, but still hadn't decided which – if any – of the candidates were worth supporting. None of these young professionals could summon up any respect for politicians. They scoffed that all politicians were inherently corrupt, only sought office to collect bribes, and had no policy ideas of their own. Cynicism was sky high!

Roman, a doctoral student who lectured in physics at a local university, was the only member of the English Club who was actively participating in the electoral process. So, on election Sunday, I met him at the poll where he was a party observer to get my first look at voting in Ukraine. A few things immediately struck me.

The ballot boxes were huge – a metre high – and clear plastic, so anyone could see the pile of ballots inside. The boxes were big because the ballots were big – the size of an 8.5-by-11-inch sheet or bigger – to accommodate the large number of candidates and parties running. And there was a line of ballot boxes because voters were choosing representatives for national Parliament, regional council, city council, and the mayor all on the same day.

I watched some older voters who had reached the front of the line head into the tall, curtained booths clutching their big bundles of colourful ballots. I also spotted an elderly couple looking overwhelmed, collapsed on chairs along the wall as they puzzled together over all these choices. But as my friends had predicted, there were few younger voters in the poll.

However, I noticed that along with Roman, several other younger people had been recruited as observers. They would have been paid, and money was very tight for young people like my English Club friends in 2002, so I doubted they were there for altruistic reasons. But they were there, and even as passive observers they made it difficult for overt manipulation to take place in the poll. After the polls closed would be a different story.

I learned later that my friends had plenty of reasons to be disillusioned, given the reputation for corruption in local politics in their city.[1] Not least among their disappointments was the fact that Eduard Hurvits, the mayor who won the most votes in Odesa in the 1998 local election, had been replaced by a decision of the courts based on a complaint brought by his main opponent, Rouslan Bodelan. All my English Club friends assumed the decision handed down by the regional Court of Appeal was politically motivated.

One way or another, Bodelan held on to the mayor's office in that 2002 vote, which explained Gene's joke. But in 2005, Bodelan in turn would be removed by a decision of the Primorsky District Court. So, one of the first things I learned about elections in Ukraine was that it's not over until it's over, and the candidate who wins the most votes is not necessarily secure in their seat. But my journey to understand elections had begun many years before.

II

I credit one of my favourite high school teachers, Mr Greenfield, for starting my career as an elections geek while I was still a teenager growing up in the eastern Ontario village of Metcalfe. I got my first taste of the ins and outs of elections and the fundamental role they play in democracy in World Politics class in grade twelve in 1978. Mr Greenfield typically delivered his lectures from behind his desk at the front of the class, formally dressed in a blue blazer with a red and white McGill University crest prominent on the pocket.

He started by teaching us that what we have in Canada is called a single-member plurality system – a first-past-the-post or winner-take-all system where the local candidate who wins the most votes is elected. In many ways, this is the simplest voting system to run. But as we have seen in recent Canadian elections, this system sometimes generates a government where the party with the most seats in Parliament hasn't necessarily won the most votes across the country. And small parties can win a lot of votes nationally without winning any parliamentary seats locally.

Mr Greenfield went on to compare the Canadian system with the proportional representation system that many European countries use. With proportional representation, voters cast their ballots for a party, and seats are allocated to members on each party list according to the percentage of votes their party got. This system is more complex, as voters rarely know who on the list will get a seat – and therefore who will represent them – until after the seats are allocated. However, it has the advantage of allowing a wider range of parties to get seats in Parliament and often leads to coalition governments.

We even had a lesson on the single transferable vote system used in Ireland. Instead of putting an "X" next to just one candidate, Irish voters can rank all the candidates on their ballot and have their second, third, fourth, etc., choices counted if their first choice isn't elected. Counting ranked votes is more complicated than the other systems, but the Irish think their system creates a parliament that reflects the electorate's will better than first-past-the-post or proportional representation.[2] In practice, there are many variations on these three systems around the world, but you don't get into that kind of detail in a grade twelve world politics class.

At the time, I liked these neat and tidy descriptions that made an election sound like a simple rules-based process where voters turn up on election day, toss their ballots in the box, and can be confident that the outcome will somehow reflect the broad will of the people.

But while I learned a lot about the technical aspects of electoral systems from Mr Greenfield, it was Bob Woodward and Carl Bernstein who opened my teenaged eyes to the kinds of corruption that can occur during an election campaign. Woodward and Bernstein's famous 1974 book, *All the President's Men* (followed by a movie version in 1976), was possibly the most influential book I read in high school – although it wasn't on the high school syllabus.[3] The bestseller laid out in great detail the investigative work by journalists that exposed US President Richard Nixon's conspiracy to subvert the 1972 presidential election and then cover his tracks. The book captured my imagination because it told more than just the story of corrupt exploits. It also explained how the pair of dogged investigative journalists conducted their research, which in the early 1970s required countless phone interviews over landlines and endless pages of notes compiled using a manual typewriter.

If Nixon's fall from grace taught me anything, it was that an election is a battle for power. It is all about the people in power fighting to hold on to that power while the people out of power struggle to wrest control away from the incumbents. That desire for power, and the control over resources that power implies, drives politicians and parties to constantly evaluate the relative costs of playing by the election rules, dancing around the rules, subverting the rules, or just plain ignoring them. So I knew that elections could be a lot more complicated than Mr Greenfield's lectures suggested, but I wouldn't fully understand what that meant in practice until I had seen quite a few elections on the ground.

In 1978 (possibly brainwashed by spending so many classes staring at Mr Greenfield's McGill crest), I left the small Ontario village where I went to high school for McGill University in the heart of downtown Montreal. Although I went on to graduate with an honours degree in political science, I focused on superpower relations in the Cold War and comparative politics in what we then called "the Third World." So I didn't come out of university understanding much more about real elections than when I went in. But I have learned a lot since then.

I've now been in and out of polls for forty years, and over the past fifteen years I've worked as a local poll official on many Canadian provincial and federal elections. But it has been my experience observing international elections that has really brought home the value of being able to freely cast your vote knowing that it will be counted correctly and that the candidate with the most votes will take office. That is not something voters can take for granted in many countries, including Ukraine.

III

I saw my first international elections up close from a village in the hill country of Sri Lanka near the district centre of Matale. I was in the country to manage a Canadian NGO's field office after building a ten-year career in international development in southern Africa and South Asia. In those years, Sri Lankan politics were notoriously turbulent. A traumatic and violent Marxist insurrection had engulfed the south of the country fewer than five years before, and there was an ongoing ethnic civil war in the northeast. In 1993, I saw provincial elections marred by the assassinations of both a prominent opposition leader and the sitting president.

However, the August 1994 parliamentary election took place in relative peace, with the newspapers noting that "only" twenty people died during the campaign. On election day, I ventured out with a co-worker, Senarath, to see what voting in rural Sri Lanka looked like. As we pulled up to his poll site, he pointed to the pavement in front of the school.

"In the last election," he told me, "this is where the insurgents wrote 'the first two people to vote will die.'"

I was shocked. "What happened?"

"When my father and I got here, there was a long line of people waiting to vote." Senarath pointed toward the building. "But nobody wanted to be the first."

"What did you do?"

"My father decided that we two would be the first ones to vote."

"Wow! And then what?"

His reply was matter of fact. "We cast our ballots. And then we went home, and we waited to see if someone would come and kill us."

In the end, Senarath and his father lived to tell the tale. But some Sri Lankans in other parts of the country were assassinated on that election day for daring to be the first at their polls to vote. And in many polls, the threat successfully deterred everyone from casting a ballot.

For my part, I have done many different things after casting my ballot in an election, but I have never spent the day waiting to see if I might be going to die because I put an "X" on that paper. Like most Canadians, I often take for granted my right to vote and to influence the composition of the government. It is hard to imagine risking our lives to vote. In fact, in recent years, nearly a third of Canadians couldn't be bothered to turn out on a federal election day – most because they felt they were too busy, or they weren't interested in politics.[4] Turnout figures are even lower for provincial and municipal elections.[5]

However, even among Canadians who are dissatisfied with government – and they may be an increasing percentage – it is rare to find people who distrust the mechanics of our elections. In fact, the reason Canadian political parties struggle to find enough volunteers to scrutinize vote counting is that people have confidence in our system. Indeed, I worked on an election in my community a few years ago where not one observer came to see the work of our five polls. A recent immigrant from the Philippines was conducting research at our site that day for Elections Canada. She was amazed at our complacency.

"In my country, the whole village would have their noses pressed to the glass outside the windows to watch the ballots being counted!" she told me.

At the end of that 1994 election day in Sri Lanka, the family I was staying with took me down to the main road after the polls closed. Crowds of local residents lined the way to observe the ballot boxes being driven from the poll to the district counting centre. As the government jeep sped past, pairs of young men on motorcycles buzzed along close behind: local party observers ensuring that the jeep took no detours and the ballot boxes stayed in sight. Everyone wanted to play their part in keeping the count honest.

IV

I have seen that passion for the democratic process closer to home, too. On 4 November 2008, I was in the New York City neighbourhood of Harlem, informally visiting polls to see how voting for the president and other races was organized in New York. It was an emotionally charged day as Barack Obama stood as the first African American to reach the ballot for a US presidential election for one of the two main parties. On Amsterdam Avenue, I spoke with an African-American man coming out of his polling station in Adam Clayton Powell Public School – a school named for the first African American to be elected to Congress from New York.

"Did you have to wait long to vote?" I asked him.

"About an hour," he replied.

"Gosh, that's a long wait, eh?" I commiserated.

He wore a look of condescension as he sized me up, a privileged white woman indulging in elections tourism. Then he simply said, "People die for this." And he went on his way.

A lot of Canadians might think he had overstated his response, but he was right. Many Canadians don't pay close attention to the voting process, but the people who run the polls know that running elections honestly is at the heart of democracy, no matter how long it takes.

V

"Are those the only shoes you brought?" I asked the young woman. It was her first time working on an election, and she was joining us for the 2018 provincial election in Metcalfe in the entry-level position of the information officer. As the central poll supervisor in my local school gymnasium, I was welcoming all the staff before the polls opened at 9:00 a.m. and preparing them for what was guaranteed to be a long day ahead before the 9:00 p.m. close.

"Oh, I'll be ok," she said. Hmmm, I thought, those little canvas shoes have no arch support. Not the best option for a job that requires standing all day. I was wearing thick-soled hiking shoes and my role didn't even involve much time on my feet. I reviewed her responsibilities, and she set off happily to welcome voters and direct them to the appropriate poll table. She was polite and enthusiastic and a great asset to our team.

"You should sit down and give your feet a break," I suggested when I spotted her later, walking around during her morning break.

"Oh, I'll be fine," she said and went back to doing her job.

Predictably, by 7:00 p.m. her feet were giving out and she was visibly hobbling. I dragged a chair into the middle of the gym at the head of the voter queue and told her to sit unless it was really necessary to get up and approach a voter. She was reluctant to be seated, but she had to finish the evening doing her job mostly from the chair. Yet she never once complained or whined. She was happy to be part of our team and, like all the other elections workers in the room, I think she realized that she was part of something important that day.

When I thanked her at the end of the day for her many hours of work, she allowed that she might wear better shoes next time. That's how I knew she would be coming back. Like thousands of Canadians, she had caught the election bug.

Elections in Canada, and around the world, depend on large numbers of ordinary citizens taking a day or more out of busy lives to run the polls, taking responsibility for understanding complex procedures and following strict rules for not a lot of pay. It is always a long and tiring day, and sometimes they have to deal with frustrated voters. But although some poll workers are retired or have part-time jobs, I have met many people who, like me, will take a vacation day from their full-time jobs for the opportunity to work on an election. Like me, they find that an election day can be the most satisfying workday of the year. That satisfaction comes from knowing that you are actively making democracy happen. Without the honest efforts of all those poll workers, democracy would just be a nice idea on paper.

This book is about how I came to observe first hand both the good and the bad – in Ukraine and in other countries – when voters who are determined to have their say meet up with poll workers who are committed to giving them that opportunity. Together, they face off with the powerful in their society, who may have quite different ideas. The lessons I learned remain relevant for Canadians today.

2   Assembling the Team

I

Long before I was seconded to my first official mission, I was already informally observing elections. While I was working on international development projects in Sri Lanka in 1991–94 and in Ukraine in 2001–02, I was already taking note of the strengths and weaknesses of electoral processes, using my camera to capture evidence and sending home detailed written reports to my family and my local community newspaper. It was clear to me that if you wanted to understand and evaluate an electoral process you needed to look beyond the technical aspects of running the polls. You had to explore the wider context, such as access to balanced information about parties and their candidates, women's involvement, youth engagement, voter intimidation, and campaign violence. So I was well primed when I discovered in the early 2000s that I could apply to be an election observer, seconded by the Canadian government to international missions.

Canadian commitment to democracy in Europe goes back to the Second World War and continued through the Cold War. Pierre Trudeau represented Canada as prime minister when the Conference on Security and Co-operation in Europe first met in 1975. Canada went on to be a member of the OSCE when it was formalized in 1995 as an intergovernmental organization with a mandate to promote stability, peace, and democracy. The OSCE's Office for Democratic Institutions and Human Rights (ODIHR) supports democratic processes in member states through initiatives such as responding to member requests for international election observation missions. Those missions often include Canadian observers.

Back in the 1990s, most of the Canadians seconded to international election missions were patronage appointees selected by the government in power, and many were bureaucrats or Elections Canada officials. After 2001, the then-Liberal government decided to move the observer selection process to an arm's-length agency. CANADEM, a non-profit, non-partisan organization, was selected to recruit and deploy qualified Canadian election observers from all walks of life.

Over the past two decades, the Canadian government has invested more than $34 million in election observation through CANADEM. During that time, CANADEM has helped the government deploy more than 3,000 election observers, including me, to serve on more than 150 multilateral and bilateral missions in more than 50 countries. The vast majority of these observers – more than 2,500 – were deployed to Ukraine on Canadian bilateral election observation missions and on missions organized by the OSCE.[1]

Many of the observers CANADEM has sent to monitor elections in Ukraine were Canadians of Ukrainian descent. During the 2106 census, about 1.25 million people in Canada identified as having Ukrainian ancestry.[2] The organizational efforts of members of this community have motivated successive Canadian governments to invest in a range of supports to Ukraine since its independence in 1991. I do not have any Ukrainian ancestors and my experience in Ukraine began almost accidentally.

In the mid-1990s, I took a five-year break from my international development career. But as the decade drew to a close, I was itching for a new adventure. I came across a volunteer opportunity in Ukraine. Given that a lot of my university studies had focused on Soviet-American relations, the thought of spending some time in one of the former Soviet republics was intriguing. I ended up on a ten-month posting in Odesa, Ukraine, working with civil society organizations and beginning to learn Russian. Then, a year later, I took a two-year job in Tajikistan, another post-Soviet republic in central Asia. My first secondments through CANADEM were on OSCE election observation missions in Tajikistan in 2006 and Kazakhstan in 2007. I got my first election assignment in Ukraine in 2010. After a return to central Asia in 2011 for elections in Kyrgyzstan, I went back to Ukraine in 2012, 2014, and 2015.

II

Walking into the first day of the long-term observer briefing in Kyiv for the 2015 OSCE election observation mission, I am overtaken by a mixture of excitement and apprehension tinged with the inevitable overlay of jet lag. I arrived in the city the day before after an overnight flight from Ottawa via Frankfurt, one of eighty long-term observers being deployed from OSCE member states in Europe, former Soviet republics, the United States, and Canada. We are all here to observe local elections being held across Ukraine.

As with the other six long-term observer missions I have been on, I had only a few weeks' notice before I left home. But, as I have been a home-based independent research consultant for some years, I look forward to international missions like this – suddenly being swept up into a large team project peopled by old and new friends, all working together on a giant puzzle that is the upcoming election.

Over the years, I have come to appreciate that an OSCE election observation mission is a complex research project with a structured methodology that requires strong working relationships and cooperation between long-term observers and other mission members. Sixteen people on the core team for this 2015 election observation mission are based in Kyiv. Half of the core team are analysts who covered politics, election administration, election law, national minorities, and the media. The other half are responsible for logistics such as staffing, equipment, travel bookings, finance, and security. I already know some of the core team from previous missions, but the first big question for me is who will be my long-term observer partner, and what are they like?

When international election observation began in the late 1950s, missions relied mainly on the observations of short-term observers who turned up a few days before election day and left a few days after. Local observers criticized these missions for having a weak understanding of the context surrounding the election and missing the kinds of manipulations that take place in the weeks or months before or after the actual voting.[3] Beginning in the early 1990s, election-observing organizations began deploying long-term observers who could provide observations over a couple of months and get a clearer picture of the broader electoral process on the ground.[4]

Long-term observers typically work in teams of two, on the principle that two pairs of eyes will be more objective than one; also, two people can handle the workload better than one. They are usually matched with a partner from a different country and, as much as possible, the aim is for gender balance. As a Canadian woman, I have always been paired with a man from a European country. Each OSCE member country has its own approach for recruiting and deploying long-term and short-term observers, so there will always be a diverse range of people on any mission. There are no age limits, but a long-term observer needs to be mature, experienced, and available for a couple of months on short notice, which may explain why many of them are mid- to late-career professionals or retired people.

The OSCE makes an effort to represent as many countries as possible in its core teams so that no one can suggest that any one country is influencing the perspective of the mission. For the same reason, it limits the participation of long-term observers from any one country to 10 per cent of the total number requested. In 2015, the initial request is for one hundred long-term observers. I am one of ten Canadians seconded for this role but a total of twenty-three countries are represented in the hotel meeting room this morning.

I pour myself a coffee from the hotel urn and make my way between the tables in search of my name card, which I know will be beside my new partner's. Matti Heinonen turns out to be Finnish, about my age – a big bear of a man with a silver military brush cut and a warm smile. He seems a bit nervous to meet me too, which is understandable. Long-term observers are usually total strangers when they are thrown together, and they have to develop a working relationship quickly. Your partner is often the first person you speak to in the morning and may be the last person you call at night. It helps if you get along.

On the whole, most do get along fine, although I have known people who were unable to work with their partner and so did not enjoy their mission or do their best work. It is always interesting at the end of the mission to see, after eight to ten weeks of working closely together six or seven days a week, which pairs of long-term observers are still good friends, and which are no longer talking to each other. There are always some of each, but I have always finished my missions on excellent terms with my partner.

Matti and I hit it off right away. He has more missions under his belt than I do, but this is his first as a long-term observer in Ukraine. I am only on my seventh OSCE long-term observer mission, but I have been in this role three times already in Ukraine. We haven't chatted for long before we head over to the large wall map to see where our area of responsibility will be. Because the second big question I always have is: where am I going to be based?

Up to now, I feel like I have worked my way around the edges of Ukraine. More than a decade earlier, in 2001–02, I worked for ten months on an NGO project in the southern Black Sea port of Odesa, and I visited the western city of Lviv and a southern resort in the Crimea. My first long-term observer assignment had been on the 2010 presidential elections in the northeastern city of Kharkiv and my second was in the east-central city of Dnipropetrovsk for parliamentary elections in 2012. In 2014 I observed a round of early parliamentary elections in the far western region around Ivano-Frankivsk. On each of these visits I also spent time in the northern capital of Kyiv. It seems somehow appropriate that for these local elections Matti and I are going to fill in a gap on my map in a region that is almost exactly at the geographic centre of the country: Kirovohrad.

Our area of responsibility in Kirovohrad includes a small city of a quarter of a million people and the surrounding region, with a total population of about one million.[5] The first basic responsibility of our team will be to spend the next five weeks gathering qualitative information about the campaign and the electoral process in our region. Our observations will be fed back weekly to the core team, who will synthesize reports from all over the country to put together a national picture of how the election is progressing.

A briefing for long-term observers is a bit like being back in university listening to lectures, right down to the fat binder full of reading materials and the inevitable too-clever student at the back of the room asking about details that no one else cares much about. But as most of the information is highly pertinent to our upcoming work, I am less inclined to nod off than I had been back in my student days.

Over the day and a half of the briefing, members of the core team, who arrived a week to ten days earlier, set out the background to this election. Inevitably, they start with recent political history, including the Euromaidan Revolution – which overthrew the previous elected president less than two years before – and the ongoing Anti-Terrorist Operation that the Ukrainian government launched in response to rebellion in the Donetsk and Luhansk regions a couple of months after that. We move on to discussions about the legal framework governing Ukrainian elections, the structure of the election administration, the media landscape, and how we will be asked to report on it all from our regions.

Our ears perk up when the legal analyst tells us to be prepared for the possibility of a second round of voting in the mayors' races. She points out that if none of the mayoral candidates get 50 per cent of the vote in the first round, the law requires a run-off election three weeks after the first election. Matti and I immediately wonder if the mayor's race in Kirovohrad will be a close one. We agree that we would not mind if our observation assignment was extended by a few weeks.

The legal analyst also briefs us on the complexities of the system for registering complaints and following them through the courts. I see that it might be complicated to keep track of all the actors who could register complaints and all the places they could register them. I file away the printout of that presentation in case we need to refer to it later.

The second day of briefing we address the other big responsibility that long-term observers take on: Matti and I will be in charge of planning and logistics for the teams of short-term observers who will join us in the field for the last few days before the election to gather quantitative data on activities in the polls on election day. We spend Saturday morning learning about logistics for short-term observers, security, and managing team finances. This is less a college lecture and more like instructions for tour guides. I am secretly hoping that Matti will take on a lot of this work, as I am not cut out to be a tour guide.

In the afternoon, we meet with the logistics team to collect our equipment. Implementing an election observation mission in a short period is a complex logistical task at the best of times. Ukrainian election missions in particular can be dauntingly large, with about one hundred long-term staff and up to six hundred regular short-term observers plus additional parliamentary observers. However, the OSCE has a reserve of experienced operations experts who are adept at quickly acquiring office space, furniture, and computer equipment, making initial travel and accommodation arrangements, and identifying interpreter assistants and drivers for forty locations around the country. Mid-afternoon, Matti and I sign for our comprehensive kit that includes a laptop with software loaded, a printer, flash drives with folders of all the basic information and documents we need to begin our work, and a late-model Android smartphone for each of us, already programed with the phone numbers of all the other mission members. We are set to begin another mission.

III

What keeps people like Matti and me coming back to these missions? To start with, over my six previous assignments as a long-term observer, I have found that an election observation mission can become – at least temporarily – your whole universe. It is an immersive experience where you are thrown into the trenches with new friends in a new city working on an all-consuming assignment where you are constantly learning something new about democracy.

Matti points out that we also enjoy a lot of privileges. We are being paid to visit new landscapes, learn about a different economy, and experience another culture. And we know that with any luck, we will also get to stay in comfortable hotels or rent a reasonable apartment, eat a lot of tasty local food, and visit museums and cultural sites. In Ukraine, you can even find yourself on an evening outing to a top-quality opera, ballet, or concert, or cheering on a lively football match.

However, we know that this is not a holiday. It is professional work with the expectation of a six-day workweek, with long hours on many days. So, although a long-term observer assignment might come with many of the advantages of a package tour, it is not the perks that keep us coming back.

"It's those women, sitting all those hours in that unheated classroom in the winter, in their fur hats and coats, way up that gravel road in that hillside village processing voters, and trying to do it all right with their limited resources," is how my friend Ted, a fellow Canadian long-term observer, puts it to me. "It's the inspiration of seeing that commitment to the democratic process! That's what keeps me coming back."

I, too, have visited many polls in rural village schools where the poll staff were mostly women teachers who were probably not given a lot of choice about taking hours away from their regular jobs to work on the election. Nevertheless, they were determined to run the poll correctly, according to the law, so that the people in their community could exercise their democratic right to vote. We would find them spending hours handwriting hundreds of voter notification slips to deliver door-to-door. We would watch them counting thousands of ballots into the early morning hours. And then hear them being scolded by higher-level election commissions when their numbers don't quite add up. In many ways they have a thankless task, and yet they stick with it, as Matti and I will soon see in Kirovohrad.

IV

"So, how many protocols will you have to fill out at the end of the counting?" I ask the chairwoman of the Novenska Settlement poll on the outskirts of Kirovohrad. The protocol is the official record of the results, or what we call the Statement of the Vote in Canadian elections.

Valentina Riabova, chairwoman at poll 350823, is gracious in answering our many questions. "Well, people here are voting for the regional council, the city mayor, the city council, a city district council, our local settlement mayor, and our settlement council," she replies, ticking them off on her fingers. "They'll get six ballots each."

"So, you have to count six races?"

"It will be more than that. The area for our settlement council is divided into nine electoral districts. So, in fact, we have to count fourteen separate races."

"Fourteen?" That's a lot, I think. The most we would count in a municipal election in my Ontario community would be six races, and in many communities we have electronic tabulators anyway.

"Yes. And then when we have the results, we will fill out the protocols. The election law says that for each race, we must write one copy of the protocol for each polling commission member – there are eighteen of us – and six copies to take up to the Territorial Election Commission. And then if there are other observers, they should each get one, too."

At this point my brain is exploding. After the voting, the poll commission members might have to hand fill and sign more than three hundred results protocols, undoubtedly in the early hours of the morning, probably after working non-stop for more than twenty hours.

"And how many voters do you have?" asks Matti.

"There are 1,714 people on our voters list."

It seems absurd. But this is the reality of the task before them. And that's what keeps me coming back: the inspiration of witnessing these ordinary people putting in an extraordinary effort to make an election happen.

A Traveler's Interlude
On the Streets of Kyiv

EARLY IN THE MORNING I go out for a stroll around Kyiv. My habit of walking the streets of any community I visit is driven by more than just a need to stretch my legs. It is part of how I build my understanding of the wider social context of an election. I find I feel at home in a new place much more rapidly when I step out and silently share the company of the early risers on their way to work. I like to quietly search for clues to the underlying economy, look for the history in the local architecture, and take in the planned and accidental green spaces. And of course, I am constantly on the lookout for signs of the current campaign at street level.

I head out the doors of the hotel while the sun is still low on the horizon. The hotel sits up on a hill above the city centre and I walk around the circular drive and turn into the shade of the narrow, tree-lined Hospitalna Street. A couple of hundred metres to the right, I pass the entrance to the Kyiv Fortress Museum, which hints at Ukraine's past within the Russian empire. Behind the gates, which are closed at this early hour, I glimpse a low, semi-circular two-story building surrounding a paved courtyard. It reminds me of Fort Henry in Kingston; not surprisingly, it was built during the same period as that Ontario fort, when Kyiv was garrisoned by the Tsarist Imperial Russian Army. This was once a military hospital that gave the street its name.

I turn left, down to Lesi Ukrainky Boulevard, named after one of Ukraine's foremost women poets, and walk almost a kilometre uphill along this six-lane boulevard. Down the centre runs a treed median that forms a narrow linear park. I pass a series of long Soviet-era nine-story apartment buildings built after much of Kyiv was destroyed in the Second World War. One of the most common and enduring forms of public art from the Soviet era is mosaics: a quarter-century after the collapse of the Soviet Union, the ground floors of these buildings are still adorned with elaborate images assembled from small ceramic tiles. The subjects seemed to be stylized people, flowers, and trees, and the palette of browns and oranges speaks to me of the 1970s. But sadly, from an artistic perspective, random parts of the larger-than-life images are now obscured or replaced by new windows and metal store entrances whose bright colours jar with the subtle older tones of the mosaics. These post-Soviet private businesses don't seem to have much respect for the integrity of outdated communist art.

At the top of the hill, I reach an open square the size of a football field in front of the building housing the Central Election Commission. Members of our core team will be in and out of this building often during the weeks ahead, observing the workings of the apex body responsible for administering the election across the country. I won't have reason to visit the building, but over previous elections I have spent many hours on the commission's website analyzing administrative information for the region I am observing.

However, the commission's offices are not my goal this morning. On the opposite side of the street, near the entrance to the Pecherska metro station, I spot one of my favourite new Ukrainian conveniences: a coffee car. A pared-down version of the Canadian food truck, the diminutive coffee car has a fully functioning European espresso machine on a shelf inside its open back doors and all the accoutrements of a mini café. This rolling coffee bar offers thirteen coffee options, much as you might find in a Starbucks, but at much more affordable prices. For ten hryvnia – less than one Canadian dollar – the young Ukrainian street barista freshly grinds some beans for a take-away macchiato, which I sip as I retrace my steps to the hotel.

3 Prepare the Field

Prepare the field → Win the votes → Buy the votes → Steal the votes → Invalidate the votes

3.1 Getting Ready to Observe

Matti and I know that long before we take the train south to Kirovohrad on that Sunday morning to begin our 2015 observation mission, local politicians and power brokers will have been preparing the field for the upcoming local elections. An election may seem like a time-limited exercise for observers or even voters, but for the people seeking power it is just another stage in a long game. We observers are arriving in the middle of that game. We will have to look carefully to get a sense of what has come before and where it is all going after voting day. Of course, as the cliché goes, all politics is local. Even in national elections, much of the real action plays out at the local level, but observing electoral politics during local elections is particularly intimate and intense. Fortunately, we won't be working alone.

When we arrive mid-morning at the Znamyanka train station that serves the city of Kirovohrad, we are met by the two other people who will fill out our four-member long-term observer team for the next two months. Our driver Anton is a gentle middle-aged man who had worked for election observers before. His suv will be essential for getting the team around the large region we are responsible for. We will rely on him to locate the many addresses we want to visit, advise us on itineraries, and get us where we need to be on time. Anton doesn't speak English, but he understands enough for the essentials. I look forward to practicing my Russian with him while Matti and Anton begin to transcend their language barrier over cigarettes in the parking lot.

But in many ways, the most important member of the team is our long-term observer assistant. The assistant's most obvious role is to interpret, as it is unusual for long-term observers to speak the local language at a professional level, and the working language of the OSCE is English. However, the assistant's job involves a lot more than just repeating what we say in Ukrainian or Russian. A lot of their formal tasks are administrative, such as helping us locate and keep track of the many contacts we need to arrange to meet. A really good long-term observer assistant goes even further, informally helping the long-term observers understand the local context. That means not only politics but also the economics, history, culture, and social life of the region. Long-term observers need to rapidly get up to speed on the local situation; the right assistant and driver can make a huge difference to quickly building an accurate picture.

I have worked with a number of assistants over the years, and they all brought different skills to the job and took away different experiences. For some, working as a long-term observer's assistant was a transformative experience. On my first mission in Ukraine in 2010, our assistant, Pavlo, was a twenty-year-old veterinary student who spoke good English because he had lived for a couple of years in Canada as a teenager. However, he cheerfully told us when we met that he never read the newspapers, had never voted, and he wasn't interested in politics at all. We had to explain to him that reading the papers would be part of his job and we hoped he would vote so we could observe at his poll. Then we warned him that we couldn't guarantee that he might not become interested in politics doing this job. Of course, by the end of two months following a hotly contested election with our long-term observer team, we had trouble getting his nose out of the newspaper and he had become something of a political junkie, fielding requests from friends on how to ensure their names were on the voters list and fighting with his mother to change the TV channel to the late-night political talk shows.

In contrast with Pavlo, our assistant in 2015, Oksana is a mature professional and mother in her mid-thirties, a petite woman with a sparkling smile and short brown hair that curls under her chin. She spent a year in Florida during high school, so her English is excellent, and she has an undergraduate law degree and a master's in teaching English as a second language. She worked for the police department for seven years, mostly managing cadet training and teaching English-language courses. Oksana also turns out to be an active user of local internet resources, which should be valuable in helping us to understand how the election is being represented online. And, fortunately for us, she has worked with election observers three times before, so she hits the ground running.

The next day, we purchase some basic office stationery and create our temporary office in the living room of Matti's hotel suite. We set up the computer and printer/scanner on the desk, print a test page, send a test email, and make our first instant coffee at our new refreshments station on the side table. With that we are ready to begin our observations.

II

Matti and I are not the only election observers monitoring the local elections in Kirovohrad. Unlike in Canada, where scrutineers (called poll watchers in the United States) are exclusively appointed to represent candidates, in Ukraine civil society organizations can also observe at the polls. There are two large national NGOs observing these elections and we meet their representatives in Kirovohrad in our first weeks on the ground.

The older organization, the Committee of Voters of Ukraine (cvu), has been monitoring elections for twenty years. They have twenty full-time staff in the region and expect to have 150 short-term observers in the polls on election day. They also have several billboards around the city, encouraging people to get out and vote. The younger organization, the Civic Network OPORA, has been monitoring elections for about half that time and has six paid long-term observers and ten to fifteen volunteers. They hope to field about forty to fifty short-term observers on election day. Both of these Ukrainian organizations are getting the bulk of their funding for observing this election from the US government.

During previous elections, Ukrainians have told me that they are suspicious about the motives of local observers who rely on foreign funding, but we find their observations objective and valuable. OPORA in particular posts frequent reports on their local website over the course of the election, which are a useful check against our own observations.

A third organization has a long-term observer team in town. The European Network of Election Monitoring Organizations (ENEMO) has fielded a pair of observers. When not on an international mission, Mikhail works for Golos, a Russian NGO that has taken on the challenging mandate of monitoring human rights and elections in Vladimir Putin's Russia. His partner Nino is from Georgia. The ENEMO mission is about half the size of the OSCE mission, with a core team of eight and fifty long-term observers across the country. ENEMO also receives foreign funding, mostly from European governments. All three organizations use similar methodologies to our mission, and we cross paths with their representatives from time to time as we start our formal observations.

III

In our first days in the city, Oksana explains that there is a referendum on the city's name running at the same as these elections. The city referendum is not part of our observation responsibilities, but results could say a lot about the bigger political divisions in the region, so we put it on our radar. The referendum options give us an overview of local history.

The city and region of Kirovohrad are currently named for Sergei Kirov, a Russian communist revolutionary. Kirov's assassination in 1934 was a catalyst for Stalin's Great Purges in the 1930s, which led to many thousands of deaths. In 2015, the Ukrainian government passed legislation that requires changing all the place names that memorialize Soviet control of the country. The names of Marx and Lenin have to be removed from many places, but Kirov is also on the list to go. The deadline for local authorities to choose a more appropriate name is November 2015, which is fast approaching.[1] The pressure is on to find an alternative name for Kirovohrad, but working through the options is like crossing a minefield. So the city government is trying to sidestep the decision by putting the question to the public.

There are seven choices on the ballot. Some of the options harken back to deep history. Blahomyr is an old Slavic name meaning "the one who brings peace." Ukrainian is one of the Slavic languages. Eksampey is attributed to the first Scythian settlement in the region, mentioned by Herodotus around 400 BC. The Scythians are mythologized as the original inhabitants of Ukraine.

Other suggestions speak to more recent Ukrainian culture and heritage. Kozatskiy means "belonging to Cossacks." Four hundred years ago, this region was the home of the Zaporizhia Cossack community. Zlatopil translates as "golden fields" in Ukrainian, calling up the image of the vast wheat fields that came to dominate this rich agricultural region in the previous century. Agriculture and food processing are still important in the regional economy. Kropyvnytskyi is the name of the founder of the first professional Ukrainian theatre, which was established in this city in 1882 and is still operating.

Inhulsk is the name of the main river running through the city. It sounds like the most neutral option, but this choice may have been tainted by the support of the ultra-nationalist parties like the Freedom and People's Control parties.

Ironically, the most controversial option is Yelisavetgrad, the name the city used for more than 150 years before 1924, which originated in the name of the local fort built by the Russians in 1754. People who want to revert to this historically Russian name claim that Fort Yelisavetgrad was named after St Elizabeth, the mother of John the Baptist, a popular saint in the Orthodox Christian canon whom both Russians and Ukrainians can revere. Ukrainian nationalists counter that the fort was named for the Russian empress Elizabeth, who established the fort to solidify her rule over Ukraine in the mid-1700s. In their view, supporting the Yelisavetgrad option is tantamount to saying you are in favour of closer ties with Russia – unacceptable, given the ongoing war.

We get a good introduction to local history as we learn about the referendum, but I know from experience that there are other ways to understand the broader historical context when you are on a new mission.

IV

In 2012, I discovered that my base in the city of Dnipropetrovsk featured prominently in a famous volume of Soviet literature. Sitting up in bed in my rented apartment with the fat red tome propped on my knees, I couldn't stop turning the pages of Alexei Tolstoy's epic novel about the Russian Civil War, *The Road to Calvary*. I hadn't realized before that evening that the plot was going to take me directly into the local history of Dnipropetrovsk in 1918. Vadim Roshchin, one of the book's central characters, had arrived at the end of the railway bridge that crosses the Dnipro River into the city at a station that we had passed through by rail only a few weeks before. Roshchin had deserted from the White Russian Army and was fighting alongside the red communist revolutionaries.

In 1918, Dnipropetrovsk – then called Yekaterinoslav after Catherine II, empress of Russia in the late 1700s – was under the control of counter-revolutionary forces. I turned the page to find Roshchin helping lead the forces of Batko Makhno, the celebrated Ukrainian anarchist, over the bridge and into the very station where we stepped down from the train and met our interpreter and driver for the first time. The station building we arrived at had been rebuilt after it was destroyed in the Second World War, but with its Greek columns and vaulted central hall, it had all the grandeur I had come to associate with old Ukrainian train stations.

On the next page Roshchin was fighting his way up Yekateriniski Prospect, the street I walked down on my way to the Academic Opera and Ballet Theatre the previous weekend. In 2012, the street still had its Soviet name, Karl Marx Prospect, but it would be given the Ukrainian name Dmytra Yarvornystkoho Avenue after 2014. The theatre was an unremarkable modernist structure, but I passed many buildings along the street whose architecture, with more of those Greek columns, pastel paintwork, and tall narrow windows suggested they had been there in back in 1918.

Finally, Roshchin and his anarchist patrol burst through the plate glass doors and sprinted up the central stairs of the Astoria Hotel, the very hotel where we had been that week to scope out accommodations for our short-term observers. I would be storming up those stairs myself in a couple of weeks to put a metaphorical bomb under the bed of a short-term observer who had overslept and was in danger of missing the early-morning train to Kyiv. Roshchin was a fictional character, but Nestor "Batko" Makhno was a historical figure who took over the Astoria Hotel for the headquarters of his Revolutionary Insurgent Army of Ukraine in 1918–19. I knew that because I had read the bronze plaque beside the hotel door. I always enjoy good literature, but there is nothing so engaging as a story that is set on the streets where you are currently living.

V

There is no requirement for long-term observers to learn much about the history of the places they visit, and many observers remain blissfully oblivious to much that occurred before the most recent election. But I think it is useful to learn as much local history as I can about any place I am visiting, and eastern Europe has a deep and complex past.

Indeed, I think it is difficult to make much sense of Ukrainian politics and culture if you don't know at least something about the episodes of unimaginable upheaval, destruction, and death that afflicted Ukraine over the first half of the twentieth century. There is plenty of academic debate about exactly how many Ukrainians met an untimely death during those fifty years, but some estimates suggest that nearly thirty million people died during a series of traumatic events that still reverberate today.[2]

It helps to understand that at the end of the nineteenth century, the lands that we now know as Ukraine were divided between the tsarist Russian Empire in the east and the Austro-Hungarian Empire in the west. Both monarchies collapsed at the end of the First World War in 1918 in the aftermath of the widespread death and destruction that occurred along what Europeans called the Eastern Front – which paradoxically ran through western Ukraine, then known as Galicia. Three and a half million people, or 12 per cent of Ukraine's population, died as a result of that war.

The Bolshevik Revolution broke out in Russia in October 1917, and big swaths of the Russian Empire became mired in a destructive civil war for several years – including Ukraine, where a number of armies fought for control and nearly four million people, or 13 per cent, died. The Bolshevik Soviet government consolidated communist control over the eastern part of Ukraine in 1921, but the far western provinces that had been part of the Austro-Hungarian Empire became part of Poland between the First and Second World Wars. As a result, the western-most provinces of Ukraine would experience about forty-five years of Russian and communist rule. In contrast, central and eastern Ukraine were under communist rule for seventy years and under Russian rule for centuries.

Directly after the civil war, there was a famine in the 1920s in the Soviet part of Ukraine and nearly three million more people died. And then, in the early 1930s, during the collectivization of agriculture, the Soviet government created the most famous famine – the one that Ukrainians call the Holodomor, or the great famine. Something like five million more people died in this famine – 17 per cent of the population.

Less than a decade later, in 1941, the whole of Ukraine was occupied by the invading Nazi German Army with more devastating consequences for the people of Ukraine. The Soviet Army began to push back the Germans in 1943, and by 1944 they reached western Ukraine and brought the whole of Ukraine under Soviet rule. An estimated ten million people in Ukraine died during this Second World War – or the Great Patriotic War, as it was called in Soviet times – which was more than a third of the Ukrainian population. A further one and a half million people died in a famine in the post-war 1940s.

So, in less than fifty years, the people of Ukraine suffered through successive waves of violence and death that included the First World War, the Bolshevik Revolution, the Civil War, the 1930s famine, and the Second World War. The second half of the twentieth century was peaceful in Ukraine, and the collapse of the Soviet Union in 1991 resulted in the independence of Ukraine. However, with the end of communism and the move towards a market economy in the 1990s, Ukrainians suffered a sustained socio-economic shock that was a new traumatic blow for the generations that had grown up after the end of the Second World War. With high death rates, low birth rates, and extensive emigration, the population of independent Ukraine shrank from more than fifty-one million in 1991 to less than forty-four million by 2022.[3]

A Traveler's Interlude
In the Suburbs of Odesa

ELECTIONS DON'T TAKE PLACE IN A VACUUM. They are steps in a long historical journey. So, from my first visit to Ukraine in 2001, I was as struck by which parts of local history were not remembered in stone and bronze as which parts were. I never saw any memorials for the people who died in the First World War, let alone the Russian Revolution or the Civil War. In my Canadian village, like most other Canadian communities, we have a memorial dedicated to the local boys who died fighting in France in the First World War. It was commissioned by the local Red Cross Committee in the early 1920s only a few years after the war's end. Most of the names of the thousands of other soldiers who died like them are carved in stone somewhere across the country, and the name of every single soldier is inscribed in the *Book of Remembrance* displayed in the Peace Tower in Ottawa. For Canada, the First World War was a significant moment of nation building, but for eastern Europe it was a time of imperial dissolution. When the Bolsheviks took power, they had no desire to commemorate the soldiers who died defending the tsar's empire, regardless of the fact that most were conscripts who had no choice in the matter. And there have been so many deaths since then that these early-twentieth-century deaths have been eclipsed.

In Odesa, I saw memorials of all shapes and sizes for the people who died in the Great Patriotic War. Continuing a long-standing Soviet tradition, newly married Ukrainian couples were still leaving their wedding flowers at the foot of these memorials as a tribute to all the people from their community who lost their lives. I found this a touching practice, but I could never get over the fact that Soviet memorials date the war from 1941 to 1945. Canadians – and many

Ukrainians – date the beginning of the Second World War to the invasion of Poland in 1939, when the German and Soviet regimes divided Poland between them, and western Ukraine first came under Soviet occupation. However, I found that it is the small, obscure, and unexpected monuments that can be the most moving.

Walking around during lunch hour near our office in Odesa, I noticed a small monument down a small side street. The size of a large tombstone, it sat in the middle of a scruffy little lawn the size of a suburban backyard, shaded by a few stunted trees with their trunks painted white to ward off insects. I couldn't understand the Russian inscription, but I recognized a Star of David at the top and a line of Hebrew script at the bottom.

The next day, I dragged my interpreter, Yulia, out to read the monument for me. Yulia was just twenty-one, with long, dark hair and dark eyes, and was prone to mischievous grins on a good day. However, she was also an emotional young woman and could slip into silent tears on a bad day. She espoused strong Christian principles, but not those of the dominant Ukrainian Orthodox Church. Yulia had honed her English skills, and her Christian values, interpreting services for American missionaries at an evangelical church.

Although she grew up in Odesa, Yulia had never heard of this monument or the story behind it. She stared at it for a moment before she translated.

"It says: 'In this place, 19 October 1941, the fascist beasts burned alive about twenty-five thousand Soviet citizens.'"

The monument looked like it had only been here since the late Soviet era, perhaps the 1980s, but even then the government was reluctant to single out the Jewish people who died in the war, insisting on subsuming them under the generic category of "Soviet citizens." But this was obviously a memorial for a massacre specific to the Holocaust. And it's uncomfortable to admit that my first reaction smacked of Holocaust denial.

"That can't be right," was the first thing that came out of my mouth. "It must say two thousand five hundred."

"No, it says twenty-five thousand." Yulia stared quietly at the stone.

"Are you sure?" My brain couldn't take it in.

"Definitely: *dvadtsat piat tysaich*. That's twenty-five thousand."

"Twenty-five thousand?"

"Twenty-five thousand."

Somehow that old adage that human bodies are 98 per cent water came to my mind. How could twenty-five thousand bodies be burned? And here? We looked around us. On one side, simple post-war houses were surrounded by flowerbeds ablaze with daffodils in the bright spring sunshine. On the other side, the roofs of small industrial buildings, including our office, could be seen over a bland concrete wall. Such a peaceful, banal place.

"And what does it say at the bottom?" The line of Hebrew was duplicated in Russian.

"At the bottom it says: 'We will remember.'"

Back at the office, I poked the internet and eventually found a short reference to the massacre in this place. Twenty-five thousand Jewish women and children and prisoners of war were locked in warehouses that were doused with gasoline and set on fire by the Romanian occupiers and their German allies in October 1941. Just one of many massacres that killed 1.5 million Jewish people in Ukraine during the Second World War. From time to time that afternoon, Yulia and I caught each other's eye across the office.

"Twenty-five thousand?"

"Twenty-five thousand."

So, in a way my first reaction was both right and wrong: what happened certainly wasn't right, but what was written was true.

3.2 Preparing the Election Administration

I

Before any election can get rolling some kind of administration must be put in place. Most countries have a permanent body responsible for election administration at the national level such as Elections Canada or Ukraine's Central Election Commission.[4] But the administrative structures that run an election at the local level are often temporary. Getting a new structure set up within a short period of time is often a scramble, and ensuring that the structure represents a wide range of political players while providing a neutral service can be complicated.

Our first full day on the job in Kirovohrad in 2015, we begin our observations at the City Election Commission. The structure of the Ukrainian election administration is inherited from Soviet days and revolves around a hierarchy of large election commissions. During local elections there are commissions set up at national, regional, city, district, and poll levels, each made up of between ten and eighteen commission members nominated by candidates and parties. In 2015, there are nearly 1,800 commissions being formed across the Kirovohrad region requiring some 25,000 commission members. But because the mayoral race in Kirovohrad city has the potential to go to a second round of voting, we know that the City Election Commission might be responsible for some of the most interesting electoral action. We start our observations there.

The City Election Commission has been allocated space in a municipal building on Dvortsova Street, one block west of the central square. This boring four-story administration building is approached by two shallow flights of steps across a nondescript plaza that blends into the street. Across the way, a more attractive formal garden fronts offices of the Ukrainian Savings Bank. Just to the right of the bank is one of Kirovohrad's fabulous art nouveau concoctions: a turn-of-the-century palace that now houses the regional museum. The museum has windows in all shapes and sizes, from tall arches to small portholes, and the walls are covered with plaster relief flowers, faces, and abstract ornaments all picked out in white paint against a pastel blue background. The window- and door-frames are works of art in themselves, with flowing curves that create a variety of organic shapes and forms in glass.

The museum building embodies those fabulously rich industrialists and their flashy show of wealth that drove revolutions before the 1920s, when the rich were stripped of their assets or exiled (or both) and these palaces were nationalized. We mentally add it to a list of places to visit soon to build a better understanding of local history.

From the outside, the renovated palace only highlights how much the utilitarian administration building across the street needs a facelift. The pavement between these two vastly different buildings morphs into a pedestrian walkway. Under the shade of mature trees, new small-scale private enterprises – trendy cafés and shops – are making a break with both the big business and big government of the past. We fortify ourselves with a cappuccino and croissant before we go in to meet the commission.

Up on the third floor of the administration building, the city commission has the use of a couple of classrooms packed with desks and fronted by a blackboard, just like high school. We stick our heads in the one they use for meetings and ask to talk with the commission leadership. There are three top members of any election commission: the chair, the deputy chair, and the secretary. This three-person team is often referred to as the *troika*. *Troika* is the Russian name of the iconic three-horse harness traditionally used to pull winter sleighs, but ironically, the term was also used for the three-man commissions – the chief of the secret police, a communist party leader, and a prosecutor – who made all the decisions at the regional level about deportations and executions in the 1930s.[5]

The *troika* of modern-day election commissions are all representatives of different parties or candidates. They usually take on this temporary election assignment alongside their day job. Of course, the more influential parties will press for their representatives in these leadership positions, or at least people who could be counted on to bend to the parties' will. At the same time, the technocrats often lobby for commission leaders who have enough experience with elections that they can manage the complexities of the election law. No one wants to see unnecessary election day complaints caused by administrative errors. An election commission *troika* doesn't have the power of the communist era *troikas*, but they hold influential positions none the less.

Sergei Osadchiy, secretary of the City Election Commission, comes out from behind his computer monitor at the back of the classroom and makes his way between the desks to meet us. In his mid-forties, Osadchiy has won his position on behalf of the Radical Party of Oleh Lyashko, which is running on a strong anti-corruption platform. Osadchiy's background is in sports. He works with a local charity that promotes football, and he is studying physical education. Perhaps this helps explain his apparent commitment to playing by the rules of the game. From this first meeting, we find Osadchiy friendly and open to frank discussions with us about the rules and who is or is not following them. He is also at pains to be clear that he is not aligned with the commission's chair, who represents the Fatherland Party, nor the deputy, who represents the president's party, the Bloc Petro Poroshenko Solidarnist (BPPS). We expect to meet Osadchiy often over the course of this election, so we hope he will continue to give us an alternative perspective on the comings and goings at the city commission.

The chairman of the commission, Mykola Chaika, has his office in the next classroom. In his early sixties, Chaika is an engineer and his day job is deputy chairman of the Federation of Trade Unions in the Kirovohrad region. He has worked on elections before, and this time he is representing the Fatherland Party. Chaika is in a delicate position, as the Fatherland Party is running a full slate of candidates in competition with BPPS candidates for all the seats on the city and district councils. But for the mayor's position, both parties have backed the same candidate. Chaika is pleasant, but we sense he is holding his cards close to his chest even before the game has started.

Oksana Frosniak, deputy chair of the city commission, is more outgoing. In her early thirties, Oksana is a good example of the post-Soviet generation of local elections junkies who work as hired guns for a range of parties. She tells us she has been a member of election commissions in the city on several previous elections, representing different parties each time. For the 2014 parliamentary elections, she was secretary for the city commission on behalf of the Party of Pensioners. She seems quite pleased with herself to have snagged a position representing the president's BPPS team in this election. She lets us know that she is confident she knows the electoral law inside out. We surmise that probably includes how to work with the law and how to work around it, depending on the circumstances.

Ukraine has an impressive range of online databases that bring together public data on political, electoral, and business registrations for individuals, providing observers with an overview of the connections between political players. Using these sources, we will see that Oksana is embedded in a local political family. Her thirty-seven-year-old husband, Vitali Frosniak, also regularly serves on election commissions and has been a candidate for local government on occasion, also representing different parties over the years. In this election, he is registered as a journalist with a BPPS newspaper, which gives him access to the polls. Vitali's thirty-one-year-old brother, Ruslan Frosniak, is the deputy chair of the city BPPS team and a candidate on the BPPS list for Leninski District Council. In June 2015, Vitali and Oksana had registered a local NGO together with their good friend Olexander Krishko. Krishko is now the chief proxy for the BPPS mayoral candidate and a candidate for the BPPS list for the Kirovska District Council. So, while she is supposed to remain neutral in her commission work, it is obvious that Oksana's family and friends are heavily invested in helping BPPS's mayoral candidate win.[6]

However, at this stage it looks like Chaika and his team have a relatively easy job. They are only responsible for forming three eighteen-member commissions for Kirovska district, Leninski district, and the small suburban settlement of Nove. At the end of the election, the city commission will total up protocols from only these three districts for each race. While there will be more work in the first round of voting than the second, overall, sitting on the city commission looks like a light assignment. It is more prestigious than serving at the district level but involves less actual work. Of course, that is if everything goes according to plan and there are no controversial complaints.

The big work in the city's election structure all takes place at the district level, and it is not evenly distributed. The Nove Commission has just one commission to deal with. Leninski District Commission has to organize forty-five eighteen-member poll commissions. Kirovska District Commission has the biggest job, organizing seventy-four poll commissions, and it's a process that requires a lot of negotiations between the parties.

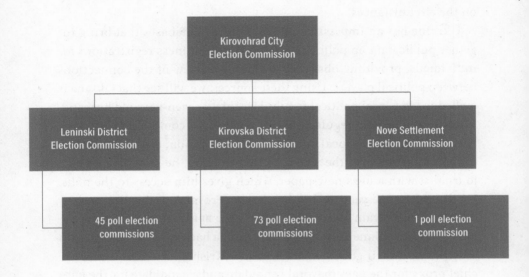

Election commission structure for local government elections in Kirovohrad, 2015.

II

"That's it?" I say to Matti and Oksana.

"It seems so," replies Oksana.

"How could they make all those decisions so quickly?" This meeting to finalize membership in a large number of poll commissions seems to be over almost before it has begun. There had been very little to observe at all. But then backroom decisions by their nature are not amenable to observation.

Some of the problems in Ukrainian elections are much the same as in Canadian elections, such as finding enough people to run the polls. And yet the poll workers who hand out the ballots to individual voters are some of the most important people in the electoral process. In the

2021 Canadian federal election, the Elections Canada office in my riding was still scrambling a day or two before voting day to find enough poll workers and get them trained for their positions in time. I see a lot of scrambling to fill poll positions in Ukraine too. Oksana showed us a Facebook post from a commission member in the Kirovohrad region begging other people to come forward and serve in the election.

When we arrived for a 5:00 p.m. meeting for the second day in a row at the Kirovska District Election Commission, officers were anticipating another long meeting. The commission has set up its headquarters on the ground floor of a two-story early-nineteenth-century building at the corner of Dvortsova Street and Dekabristiv Boulevard that sports a well-maintained exterior but is run down inside. The commission's main office is a long, high-ceilinged room with a parquet floor, embossed plaster tiles on the walls, and windows that look out on a dim interior courtyard.

The chair of the commission, Lubov Yarysh, is a stern, no-nonsense woman in her fifties who looks like a schoolteacher who spends much of her day disciplining wayward teenagers and wouldn't hesitate to use those skills on her election assignment, if necessary. The deputy chair, Oleksander Bezzubov, is a smoother character – a lawyer who represents the BPPS. The secretary, a middle-aged woman named N.P. Lokareva, is quietly focused on recording the proceedings. As we take our seats this Friday afternoon, Yarysh and Lokareva are barricaded behind their computer monitors at desks at the far end of the room. A tall metal safe looms in the corner behind them, safeguarding commission papers from prying eyes. The chairs for observers and media are set up in rows down the other end of the room, leaving an open space in the middle where meetings and other activities take place.

The meeting the day before had been quiet and orderly as we watched the commission run a series of lotteries to determine who would sit on commissions for the three-quarters of the district's polls where a surplus of commission members had been proposed by the parties. In a public and transparent process, a commission member pulled numbered Ping-Pong balls out of a drum to choose commission members from numbered lists for each poll. For the other quarter of the polls, a minimum number of commission members or fewer had been nominated, so a lottery wasn't necessary. At the end of the meeting, the chair told us to come back at 5:00 p.m. the next day if we wanted to see the final stage of the process.

This second evening the commission needs to finalize who will lead each poll commission as chair, deputy, and secretary. As the district needs to balance party representation with adequate experience working on elections in each *troika*, these decisions are bound to be more subjective and political, and might be expected to take some time. We also heard before the meeting that about ten poll commissions still lacked enough ordinary members to meet a 50 per cent quorum. At the same time, there is a legal deadline looming at midnight to finalize commission lists fifteen days before election day. We expected that the district commission members would engage in some complex negotiations, and we had been instructed by the core team to observe how they did that.

This is why I am surprised when the meeting goes quite quickly. Soon after the meeting comes to order, the executive presents a prepared list of recommendations for all the poll leadership positions. The executive also offers up an additional list of poll commission members they have identified who haven't officially been nominated by any party but who are available to fill the outstanding commission positions. It looks like any negotiating about the poll leadership positions has taken place earlier in the day, away from the prying eyes of observers, the media, or any party or candidate that had failed to get a seat among the eighteen district commission members.

However, if the commission chair, Yarysh, was hoping for a slam dunk, she doesn't quite get it. Two people repeatedly and loudly complain about the lack of transparency in the process. One is a commission member who represents the fiery anti-corruption politician Oleh Lyashko and his Radical Party. The other is a proxy for an independent mayoral candidate, Artyom Strizhakov. The executive's prepared lists are defended by the deputy chair, Bezzubov, who aggressively shuts down the complaints and even threatens that he has the authority to remove Lyashko's member from the commission. This back and forth gets a bit chaotic, but when the proposed lists are brought to a vote, only Lyashko's commission member votes against the proposed nominations. The rest of the district commission is solidly behind the back-room deal.

We shouldn't have been surprised, as this approach is common right up to the national level. It echoes old Communist Party approaches to decision making where the party executive made decisions behind closed doors and the wider membership was expected to rubber-stamp prepared resolutions. After the 2014 presidential election, our core team elections analyst noted: "As in previous elections, the [Central Election Commission (CEC)] held unannounced 'preparatory' meetings prior to sessions."[7] The CEC would then get unanimous uncontested support from the commission in public for resolutions that had been sorted out earlier at the private meetings. The public vote provided an illusion of transparent decision-making, but the reality was much murkier.

Of course, in many ways this initial round of decision making about poll commission membership is just the beginning. Everyone knows that many of the people listed will decline their positions due to the low pay and the large time commitment, or be moved around by their parties. Numerous changes to poll commission membership up to the deadline before election day is something of a tradition in Ukrainian elections. In 2015, up to half of poll commission members will be replaced at least once in some regions of the country.[8] The horse-trading at Kirovska district is just getting started.

Meanwhile, within two days the members of the new poll commissions will come together across the district and begin their work. Before election day they are responsible for distributing invitations to voters, making the voters list available to the public, displaying basic information about the candidates and parties, and arranging the tables and voting booths at the poll site. On election day they will be managing the voters lists and ballots during voting. Then they will count the ballots after the close of the polls and take protocols of their results to the district commission for tabulation. And, if there are formal complaints about any of their work, the poll commission will have to consider those complaints and make decisions in response. Their jobs will continue over the two weeks before the election, and up to five days after the official announcement of results by the Central Election Commission. It is no small task, and I have a lot of respect for the women – and they are predominantly women – who take it on.

A Traveler's Interlude
In the Churches of Kharkiv

IF YOU WANT A DEEPER UNDERSTANDING of the culture of a new country, you do well to learn something about local religious expression. The real passion of our assistant in Ivano-Frankivsk was painting churches, a vocation handed down to him by his father. Petro was a serious forty-year-old with a steady gaze and thinning, but still black, hair combed back from his forehead. Being a devout Orthodox Christian was an essential part of his Ukrainian identity and painting was his way of helping the church reach out to vulnerable Christians.

The interior walls of Orthodox churches are traditionally painted with scenes from the Bible and stylized portraits of saints and holy figures. Smaller icons painted on wooden panels are also hung on the walls. After emerging from the religious repression of the communist era, many communities in this western Ukrainian province were rebuilding or renovating their churches, and there was a demand for artists with more than technical abilities. Petro told us that decorating a church was a spiritual practice. He didn't just turn up with his paint and brushes and dash off a picture; he had to enter a contemplative frame of mind and spirit to produce an image that would inspire devotion.

Coming from a Protestant background, I had seen few images in the Ontario churches I had visited, where there was a strong emphasis on the text of the Bible. So I experienced the first Orthodox churches I entered as a shock to the senses: a blaze of bright colours highlighted by the gleam of gold leaf among stands of glowing candles. In earlier times, when the ordinary peasant couldn't read text, these Orthodox church buildings functioned as a kind of four-walled graphic novel or teaching aid where, under the guidance of their priests, parishioners became adept at reading the traditional imagery on the walls and in the painted icons. These holy images only heightened the impact of the ethereal voices of the Orthodox liturgy.

Earlier, during my time in Kharkiv in 2010, many Sundays I visited the Annunciation Cathedral, a massive brick building pinned to the ground beneath an eighty-metre bell tower, to listen to the music of the liturgy. The cathedral in Kharkiv was not particularly old – it opened in 1901 – but it had not been torn down by the Soviets, as had so many other Ukrainian churches in the 1930s. In the winter of 2010, it was a bustling space.

I found the service refreshingly open and unstructured. It didn't seem to matter that I had arrived in the middle of the service – like I had arrived in the middle of the electoral process – and I mingled easily with the people coming and going. Some worshippers filtered forward to find a place in the rows of congregants standing before the priest under the tall dome at the centre of the church. Others lined up to say private prayers in front of one of the many icons hung around the large pillars that led the eye up the painted ceiling. They nodded and crossed themselves repeatedly before leaning forward to kiss the glass that protected the sacred image. With appropriate mystery, the priest emerged and disappeared through a door in the iconostasis, a towering screen that separated the altar from the nave, constructed from stacked rows of painted icons housed in a glittering gold framework. Resting on benches along the side of the nave, old ladies in floral headscarves chatted quietly, and near the back entrance a young woman stood behind the counter of a small shop selling religious tracts, candles, and reproductions of icons. Off to one side, a table was piled with loaves of bread.

I wandered around, looking at the icons as I listened to the singing. The Orthodox liturgy is choral, chanted and sung by the priest with backup from a choir divided into two groups; one group of women and men stood around a circular music stand on a ground-level dais and threw their voices up, while the other group sang down to them from a balcony above. There were no instruments inside the church, but outside there were the bells.

One Sunday, we drove south from Kharkiv to the Sviatohirsk Cave Monastery, a 400-year-old Orthodox complex built into the forested cliffs overlooking the Siverskyi Donets River. As I stood outside the Sviato-Pokrovska Church bell tower, I watched a monk in the belfry far above, dressed all in black and playing the local version of a carillon by pulling handfuls of strings attached to bells of different sizes and notes. The sound was transcendent, but inevitably, the strange dance of the monk brought to my mind the image of an oligarch pulling strings in the background of a Ukrainian political process. Sundays could be a pleasant escape from the busy round of interviews and meetings, but politics were always floating in the back of my mind. Come Monday, we would dive back into the fray.

3.3 Preparing the Voters Lists

I

One of the most important things a government does to prepare the field for an election is put together the voters list. The quality of the voting process is irrelevant if you don't start with a comprehensive list of all the people entitled to vote. When inaccurate lists have fuelled corruption in the past, building and maintaining trust in the voters lists can be an uphill battle.

"The original list of addresses I gave the District Election Commission included all those new buildings," Andriy Andriyenko told us, pointing out the addresses on the computer printout. The head of the Voter Registration Department for the town Oleksandriya in the Kirovohrad region was visibly frustrated. An article in the local paper for this small town of 72,000 voters, the Gorodskoi Kurier, had alleged that people living in these new buildings would be left off the voters list. It wasn't true.

"Did the journalist ask you before he wrote that?" I asked. I wondered who had paid for this article. Did they have an agenda that would benefit from disinformation, or did they just not know?

"No, he never talked to us. I don't know where he got his information, but it was wrong. I've asked his editor to correct the mistake now. But that article has already been copied onto several other internet sites with the wrong information."

I sympathized with his concern. The State Voter Register was one of the best success stories in electoral reform that I observed in Ukraine, but many people remained suspicious about the lists. Over the four elections I observed, I interviewed many women like Andriy's assistant, Tetiana Pylypenko, the specialist at the Oleksandriya voter registration office. They were universally diligent and professional in their work, updating the national voter database monthly, removing people who had died or moved away, and adding those who had turned eighteen or moved into the district. They worked away quietly in obscure local government offices across the country, drawing little attention but providing a vital input to any democratic election: accurate voters lists.

Inaccurate voters lists were one of the major complaints that under-mined confidence in the 2004 presidential elections and led to the Orange Revolution. In 2004, voters lists were prepared by local governments and corrections and changes were done in different ways in different areas. Multiple agencies were involved with too much of the work done manu-ally. Election officials in 2004 reported dead people on the list, errors in residency, multiple registrations for the same person, misspelled names and addresses, and entire buildings full of voters missing. Errors such as these could facilitate vote stealing by allowing ineligible people to cast ballots or they might disenfranchise legitimate voters.[9]

By 2015, the Ukrainian State Voter Register had been generating vot-ers lists for five years from a national database of all citizens who were eighteen years and older. This was a big improvement. Starting around 2007, and supported by international donors including the Canadian government, Ukraine created a centralized national register which was passive – eligible citizens were automatically included – and drew on existing administrative data. In 2010, we saw Canadian fingerprints on this system in every voter registration office we visited. Off in a corner or in a backroom we would find the same large format printer bearing a sticker with a bright maple leaf flag giving notice that they had been paid for with Canadian tax dollars. Those hundreds of printers distributed across the country were an essential technology to produce the two sets of voters lists needed in each poll. The first lists had to be in the polls early in the campaign so that voters could check if their name was on the new list. A second updated version was issued just before election day for use during voting. Going forward, local voter registration offices could generate accurate voters lists for poll commissions whenever they were needed.

Given years of experience with poor voters lists, a residual lack of trust in the lists continued to reverberate through the electoral system for several elections after the State Voter Registration was up and running. As long-term observers, we frequently heard complaints, like the one the journalist had voiced, that the voters lists had significant mistakes. However, when we challenged the people who complained to us, none had ever actually visited their local voter registration office to see how the system worked. And when we asked the voter registration employees if any political stakeholders apart from individual voters had visited to see their work, their answer was universally "no." Without those first-hand observations, it was a slow process to build trust in the system. By 2015, local confidence in the register and the voters lists was increasing, but international observers were still the only people who bothered to see for themselves.

II

If you want to measure a country's real commitment to democracy, you need to look at whether the most vulnerable people are included in the voters list, have access to a poll, and can vote in secret. For example, it is a common criticism of democracy in the United States that in many states people who have been convicted of a felony are barred from the voters list, both while they are in prison and after their release. In 2020, an estimated 5.2 million Americans were disenfranchised due to a felony conviction, or about 2.3 per cent of the potential electorate.[10] In Canada, all prisoners got the right to vote only in 2002.[11]

To the credit of Ukrainian democracy, there are no legal barriers to prevent prisoners from voting. In 2012, there were more than 150,000 prisoners in Ukraine and special polls had to be set up in each prison for them to vote.[12] However, at special polls in prisons, and in other institutions such as hospitals and military bases, there was always concern that residents could be manipulated to vote a certain way by the people in charge, usually employees of the government. However, it was very difficult to prove that pressure had been applied. During the 2012 election, my Dutch partner, Bart, was particularly interested to see the preparations for the election inside the local lock-up, so we were excited when the prison officials agreed to give us a tour of the Dnipropetrovsk State Prison.

The prison building was old – built in the tsarist era before the 1917 communist revolution, judging by the brickwork. As we were escorted down the empty corridors, my thoughts wandered to the many political prisoners who had walked these same hallways over the past century. There was little of what we would have considered justice for those who opposed the government in either the tsarist or the communist days, and prisoners under those regimes certainly didn't have access to a free vote. The parts of the building we passed through now were clean and well maintained and nothing really spoke of the totalitarian past. But we were not permitted to speak with any inmates, so there was no way to quickly judge the real conditions.

It was a week and a half before election day, and, in accordance with the law, the poll was already set up in a separate room. (In Canada, we don't set up our polls until the morning of the election.) The poll commission, made up of prison employees, seemed familiar with all the regulations. They told us their instructions were to take the prisoners to vote in alphabetical order instead of by floor, as they had done in previous elections. This meant it would take most of the day to individually walk each man through the voting process, but they looked well organized, and we couldn't find fault.

After half an hour, we were on our way out of the building. Or, rather, we were trying to leave the building. The governor of the prison was rattling away at the lock on the door with his keys, but it wasn't budging. Kateryna and I quietly exchanged glances, but we restrained ourselves from giggling. It was ironic to find ourselves locked inside the prison along with the governor, but he clearly did not see any humour in the situation.

Then, to make matters worse, the door at the top of the stairs above us flew open with a loud clang, and a guard appeared at the head of a column of young male prisoners. Some Russian words were quickly exchanged and then the young men marched down the metal stairs. They weren't wearing uniforms, but they were all dressed in similar shorts and T-shirts with their hair uniformly shaved close to their skull. As the young men approached us at the foot of the stairs, our entourage of prison officials spontaneously formed a wall in front of our interpreter Kateryna and me, pushing us out of sight into the corner.

I doubt that these men were concerned about the young prisoners encountering a fifty-two-year-old woman in wool trousers and sensible shoes. However, Kateryna was a tall, stylish Ukrainian woman the same age as these boys, and in keeping with 2012 fashions, her figure-hugging mini-skirt and a trendy little jacket left little to the imagination. With her long legs well hidden behind the wall of guards, Kateryna and I peered curiously over their shoulders as the prisoners marched sharply down the stairs and around the corner past us. Their eyes were averted, but no doubt they were wondering what had brought a lovely young woman like Kateryna into their prison.

As the young men disappeared down the corridor as quickly as they had appeared, I tried to keep a neutral face. I could see that this was just adding to the embarrassment for the governor of the prison. After some sharp discussion with his colleagues, he led us down the corridor where the prisoners had gone, and we finally exited through another door. It was a funny way to end an otherwise uneventful tour, but it hinted that what we had been shown was a superficial view of the reality inside the prison.

We assessed that it would take observers at least half an hour to get into the poll and another twenty minutes to get out (providing the doors could be unlocked ...), making an election day visit too time consuming for our short-term observers. So, the only way to assess how free the vote was would be through the actual results.

Back in 2010, when I observed the elections in Kharkiv, after the first round of voting we saw that support for the Party of Regions candidate Viktor Yanukovich was uniformly high across the whole region. At that time, the Party of Regions was a well-organized political machine that promoted a leftist ideology and supported Russian language rights and closer economic ties with Russia, and they had done well in previous elections in the east. So we were surprised to see a small number of polls showed disproportionately high support for the Fatherland Party's candidate, Yulia Tymoshenko. The Fatherland Party's base was predominantly in the west of the country where many saw it as the more Ukrainian- and European-leaning option. When we asked the District Election Commission chair if she could explain the anomaly at these isolated polls, she simply said, "Well, those polls are in prisons." She didn't have to say anything more. We knew that the prisons were administered by the Ministry of Justice, and the minister of justice reported to the prime minister, and the prime minister was Yulia Tymoshenko. We had no idea whether Tymoshenko had specifically instructed the prison governors to round up the vote in her favour or if the officials just assumed it would be expedient to show their loyalty by ensuring that their prison population voted for her. But it looked like many prisoners didn't think they had a choice.

When the 2012 results came out, I carefully checked the results from all the special polls in our region, including prisons and hospitals. Turnout at all the special polls was high. At most special polls, 90 per cent or more of voters cast a ballot, while turnout at regular polls hovered around 50 per cent. The ruling Party of Regions got between 18 and 40 per cent more votes at special polls than in regular polls, while opposition parties had consistently fewer votes. It was clear that the staff running special polls in institutions made it easy for everyone to vote, if not actually encouraging them. However, it was impossible to say whether the higher results for the Party of Regions were due to pressure on the voters, or just the higher turnout. But we could see that enough people voted for opposition parties in every institution to suggest that there was no problem with the secrecy of the vote. As it was, our calculations suggested that the Party of Regions gained more than 3,500 votes at special polls such as prisons and hospitals within the city of Dnipropetrovsk – votes that they might not have got at regular polls – but this gain would not have altered the overall results in this city as none of the races were close.

As in 2010, in 2012 we could be sure that prisoners were able to vote. But we could only infer that prisoners remained vulnerable to pressure. Another group that was alleged to be vulnerable was the homeless.

III

As I adjusted the gas under the frying pan in my Dnipropetrovsk apartment, I turned from stirring my vegetables to check the screen of my laptop, propped up on the kitchen table. It was a bit surreal, observing a poll in the middle of cooking dinner, but in the 2012 parliamentary elections, people all over Ukraine were observing from their homes. For this election, the government had invested 100 million euros to install a webcam at every polling station in the country so that anyone with internet access could see what was going on during voting.[13] The camera in poll 121326 was installed in a corner near the ceiling, so I couldn't see a lot of detail. But I could definitely see what wasn't there.

I had chosen poll 121326 to watch because the opposition parties had complained that 700 homeless people were registered at this poll. A candidate from the Fatherland Party alleged that these people might not really be homeless. Or, on the other hand, if they were homeless they would be easily bribed to vote for the ruling party. Our interpreter, Kateryna, told us that the candidate was using derogatory language when he talked about these homeless people. He certainly seemed to think it was a bad idea to have such vulnerable people on the voters list. However, ensuring that all qualified voters are on the list is fundamental to democracy, and that includes the homeless. However, it is a complicated process to ensure voting rights for people who have no fixed address. Elections Canada runs outreach programs in cooperation with homeless shelters, but they usually require homeless people to register at the poll on election day, rather than adding to the voters list in advance.[14]

When Bart and I visited poll 121326, we could see that there were indeed 700 people with the same address on the voters list, so we agreed that this deserved an investigation. When we got to the address on Sverdlova Street, an office on the ground floor at the back of a dingy Soviet apartment block, it turned out to be Dnipropetrovsk's Municipal Centre for Social Support. Deputy Director Lyudmila Matyanova was happy to set us straight.

"Part of our job is to help people who don't have a *propiska*," she explained. The *propiska* was a government stamp in their internal passport – the primary ID document in Ukraine – registering them to a specific address. "We can provide anyone in the city who is homeless a special certificate giving them this address so they can get a registration stamp at the passport office."

"Do a lot of people use this service?"

"Last year, when we could only issue a one-year temporary certificate, we had about 500 people. But this year people can get a permanent registration this way. So, our numbers have gone up to about 700." Which matched the numbers on the list at poll 121326.

"So, it's a popular service?"

"Yes, it's very important for these people. Without a *propiska* there are a lot of government services that you can't access."

"Such as getting on the voters list?"

"Yes, including getting on the voters list. Once they are registered at this address, they are automatically added to the voters list."

"And what kind of people typically need this service?"

"Mostly they are poor or vulnerable people. There are lots of reasons they are homeless. They might be sleeping rough or couch surfing. Or they could be young people who have recently graduated from an orphanage.[15] Or people who have been released from prison. And we have some Roma in Dnipropetrovsk who have never been registered. A few are just people who are between apartments. They might have sold their apartment and haven't bought a new one yet. They could need help getting a temporary registration too. We help people in all these situations get a registration."

"How do you know the system isn't being abused?"

"Well, about 80 per cent of our clients have some kind of documents. The other 20 per cent have no documents at all. The passport office checks all the names to be sure they aren't registered somewhere else already."

We listened with interest. It was a good system for helping homeless people get their official ID. But it was also a system that could be exploited during an election. Vulnerable homeless people might be encouraged or helped to register and then instructed or bribed to vote for the people who helped them. However, it sounded like getting someone registered to vote here who was also registered somewhere else would require considerable collusion.

On the other hand, as there was only one social support office serving a city of a million people, many of the people registered through this address probably stayed far from the poll that served the address. They were on the voters list, but that did not mean they had easy access to their poll. Few people would cross the city just to vote. That could leave a lot of unused ballots at poll 121326 for the unscrupulous to take advantage of. Still, getting those ballots marked and in the ballot box would require collusion among everyone in the poll – staff and local observers – so it didn't seem very likely. We decided to monitor that poll on election day anyway to see if there was unusual activity.

So, while Bart and all the short-term observers were out visiting other polls in person, I stood in my kitchen cooking and watching the end-of-day voters moving in and out of poll 121326. Were a lot of people who might – or might not – be homeless brought into the poll all at once? Was anyone stuffing the box with multiple ballots? I didn't see any sign of either. And we heard no further complaints from party observers who were in that poll. So, with the webcam oversight, we could eliminate another spurious complaint from our list.

The OSCE Final Report for that election said that many people questioned the usefulness of the webcams, but I thought they were a valuable addition. Although I couldn't argue with the fact that they were expensive to install. The money might have had more impact elsewhere, such as training in-person observers. I never saw webcams used in subsequent Ukrainian elections. So, while the cameras may have reduced corruption during voting, I had to wonder whether there was any corruption in disposing of those millions of euros of hardware.

As it was, the work of the Social Support Centre did help vulnerable people get on the voters list, but it didn't help many of them cast their vote. It was a partial solution at best.

IV

By 2014 a new vulnerable group was on the radar of election observers like me, based in the western region of Ivano-Frankivsk for the parliamentary elections that year. Although the conflict in eastern Ukraine was still in its early stages by October 2014, the fighting had already created nearly 430,000 internally displaced persons (IDPs). About two thirds of those were adults. A potential 284,000 voters were away from their normal voting place and would need to be added to the voters list in their new location if they were going to vote in these parliamentary elections.[16] The right of IDPs to vote was something OSCE was very interested in monitoring. Theoretically, IDPs from Crimea, Donetsk, and Luhansk should have been able to temporarily transfer their voting address at any voter registration office, but there was little voter information about this campaign produced nationally. We were tasked with asking local government about IDP numbers and asking voter registration offices how many IDPs were taking up the option to register to vote locally.

On our first out-of-town road trip, we arrived at the Nadvirna district voter registration office on the main street of Bohorodchany after lunch. We surprised the manager, Nadia Tytysh, but she welcomed us. Like other voter registration offices I had visited, no one apart from voters had visited her to see how her work was going, and she was happy to share what she was doing. She was very familiar with the challenges of helping IDPs change their address for the election.

"I did an interview with the local press about it," she told us. "And we have added a section to our district website with instructions for IDPs."

"Have many IDPs come in, then?"

"We had maybe twenty or thirty last week."

It wasn't a large number, but it showed us that the system was working. In fact, across the country, nearly 200,000 people temporarily changed their voting address in 2014, but fewer than 40,000 were from Crimea, Donetsk, and Luhansk. Our core team felt that a national publicity campaign could have increased the number of IDPs who voted.[17]

In 2015, IDPs are considered temporary residents and are not eligible to vote in local elections. By November 2015, their numbers have grown to 1.6 million, but none of them are on the voters list.[18]

A Traveler's Interlude
On the Streets of Kirovohrad

WITH A MISSION of only a couple of months, I want to get in touch with the local community in Kirovohrad as fast as I can. After a couple of nights in the hotel, I rent a recently renovated bachelor apartment on the fourth floor of a five-story Soviet apartment block, not far from Matti's hotel. The main room has a wall of windows that look out into the leafy tops of mature trees that surround the building and turn an otherwise drab structure into an oasis of greenery. The kitchen is cheery and full of sunshine in the morning. I find the apartment a pleasant refuge to come home to after a long day's work. Despite their utilitarian appearances, buildings like this were also a refuge for their first residents, who often moved in from the overcrowded dormitories and communal flats that many Ukrainians had been condemned to live in after so much housing was destroyed in the first half of the previous century.

Most mornings before we begin our work, I walk down Kirova Boulevard to the river. On the way, I pass more grey Soviet apartment blocks; interspersed between them are individual brick houses that probably predate the First World War. I have seen homes like this across the former Soviet Union: one-story houses built up against the sidewalk with an almost square layout and shallow peaked roofs with brick chimneys poking through. Invariably, they have rows of uniform tall, narrow windows in each wall with multi-paned wooden frames (sometimes these had been updated with vinyl windows). The wooden windows are doubled against the winter cold, usually with one small pane – a *fortochka* in Russian – that can be opened for ventilation even on cold days.

Some of these houses are plastered smooth, but many still show detailed brickwork around the windows and under the roof's overhang, echoing the decorative wood trim on traditional village cottages – called *khata* in Ukrainian – and suggesting that the city was home to many skilled bricklayers a century before. The conductor heads that top the downspout from the eaves troughs are often remarkable concoctions of ornate metalwork that add to the charm of these small homes. Occasionally, I have been lucky enough to get inside houses like these; I find that the ceilings are tall by Canadian standards, and the old plaster walls undulate and are sometimes covered with carpets for warmth and decoration. Traditionally, a round brick stove built at the intersection of the main rooms radiates heat throughout the house when it is fired up.

The Inhulsk River is narrow where I cross the bridge, confined within its banks by low concrete walls. It is always quiet in the early morning as I crunch along the gravel pathway, and the old men with their fishing lines don't disturb the mirror surface of the water as it reflects the apartment blocks upstream. Before I turn to recross the river, I pass a war memorial of four super-sized bronze soldiers carrying a wreath on their shoulders. This is the first memorial I have seen for Soviet soldiers who were sent abroad to fight in foreign wars in Eurasia, America, and Africa, although I have seen memorials before for veterans of the 1980s Soviet war in Afghanistan.

On the other side of the river, I head back uphill along the main drag, Bolshaya Perspectivnaya. On the right is the Regional Arts Museum, a grand three-story edifice with art nouveau details that suggest it was designed in the first decade of the previous century. The street-level facade has been compromised by modern shop windows, but above them some of the arched windows are still framed by balconies with whiplash curves in their iron railings, and an eccentric Moorish arch shows where the central entrance had been before a jewellery shop was inserted in the frame.

Opposite the museum is the entrance to the main bazaar, where a combination of indoor and outdoor stalls offer all kinds of food and household products. It is mostly shuttered this early in the morning, but I will be back on the weekend to do my shopping. I continue up the street past a park and city hall to where the asphalt gives way to cobblestones beside the city's central square – or *maidan*, in Ukrainian.

The Kirovohrad *maidan* is the size and shape of a football field, paved with pink and white bricks. Along the opposite side is a long, bland building that houses the regional administration, the epitome of the faceless bureaucracy. This *maidan* was the site of many days of local demonstrations during the national Euromaidan movement in 2013–14. In front of the government building is an empty plinth where the statute of some Soviet icon was taken down at that time. The marble base of the monument is now repurposed as a memorial to the martyrs who died in the Euromaidan demonstrations in Kyiv. The square looks like the obvious site for political rallies and concerts during an election and there are already pop-up tents here where candidates or parties hand out campaign literature.

At the top of the square, I turn right along Dvortsova Street to Kirova Street and head up to my apartment to get ready for the day's work.

3.4 Preparing the Candidate List

I

While the government is compiling voters lists and setting up the election administration, political parties are preparing their candidate lists for the ballot. The names that end up on the ballot are rarely a straightforward choice. The presidential election I observed in Tajikistan in 2006 was a great example of how a candidate list can be manipulated.

My Danish long-term observer partner, Connie, and I were on the road early on a warm October morning in the southern Tajikistan region of Qurghonteppa. Accompanied by our interpreter assistant, Baharudin, we were looking for some clarity about the candidates running in this election. The incumbent president of Tajikistan, Emomali Rahmonov, had been preparing the field for this election for more than a decade. As he cemented his place as leader of this small post-Soviet central Asian republic for fourteen years, it was widely understood that anyone who could have presented a legitimate challenge to his presidency by now was either in prison, in exile, or dead. Yet there were five candidates running against him, although if these five had any real campaign activities, they were almost invisible to us.

Baharudin was a short, compact young father who we had "borrowed" from the local office of a French NGO for the duration of the election. His father was a Tajik Sunni from the plains of Tajikistan, while his mother was a Shia Ismaili from high in the Pamir Mountains. His hybrid background seemed to give him a broader outlook on his society than the typical monocultural Tajiks, who rarely socialized outside their communities. Like most Tajiks who worked in professional positions at international NGOs, he was fluently multilingual in Tajik, Russian, and English. He also had enough basic Uzbek to get by and probably learned one of the obscure Pamiri languages from his mother. Listening to Baharudin set up meetings for us with his tiny 2G Nokia phone – state-of-the-art in 2006 – glued to his ear, I noticed for the first time how spoken Russian is pitched distinctly lower than Tajik or English. Flipping between Russian and Tajik, depending on the preference of the person on the other end of the call, his voice rose or fell with the language, his Tajik sounding almost squeaky compared with the sonorous depths of his Russian.

Baharudin had tracked down the local office of the Socialist Party that had nominated Abdulhalim Gaffurov as its candidate. We met Dilbar, the Socialists' provincial representative, inside the down-at-heel Soviet-era Professional and Technical School No. 9. She told us that her party didn't have a budget for campaigning across a province this large and had not scheduled any campaign events. We asked to see party campaign materials, but there were no brochures or party swag on hand. She could only show us the standard poster about her candidate provided by the Central Election Commission. The party didn't look like much of a going concern to us, and I felt embarrassed to challenge her further, but it was our responsibility to probe a bit.

"Perhaps you can tell us how your party's platform is different from the president's platform?" I inquired. I wanted to phrase the question in a non-confrontational way, but you could never tell how it would come across in translation.

Dilbar hesitated and looked extremely uncomfortable. "I don't know how to answer that," she finally replied. "The president brought us peace," she added by way of explanation, invoking his role in the peace accords that had ended the civil war a decade earlier. Clearly, she didn't want to risk criticizing the president to international observers, even though her party's candidate was ostensibly running in opposition to him.

Later in the day, we tracked down Khaydar from the Social Democratic Party in his office at Qurghonteppa University. His party had declined to nominate a presidential candidate, and he was more blunt. He presented us with a good news/bad news story. The bad news was that we saw no visible campaign because there was no real competition. "All the parties that have put forward candidates have been organized by the government," he explained. "They're not real opposition parties." However, the good news was that he didn't anticipate any election fraud. "There's no need to cheat when there is no real competition!"

A couple of days later, we conducted our own mini poll to test the public's knowledge of these non-candidates. Working with our backup interpreter, Manzura, I found a wall in the bazaar displaying the five posters issued by the Central Election Commission to publicize the five candidates running against the president. Then we strategically positioned ourselves just to one side of the posters and questioned twenty people walking by. Almost everyone we talked with knew the date of the upcoming election, planned to vote, knew where their poll was located, and was confident that their name was on the voters list. It seemed they were well prepared for this election.

However, when we asked them if they could name the parties and candidates on the ballot, despite the clues offered by the posters behind us, only two out of twenty could name more than one candidate – the incumbent. The people over age forty could name two to four parties, but only the ones that had been active in the previous election. Many of the younger voters couldn't name any parties, and nobody could name the two parties that had been created just before this election.

However, only one person suggested they were in any way dissatisfied with the election process, and several specifically said they didn't want to change their president. Which may explain why turnout on election day a week later was reported to be more than 90 per cent, giving Rahmonov 79 per cent of the votes. Although with no centralized voters list, it would have been difficult to verify the numbers released by the government.

So, better the devil you know than the one you don't, we suspected. After all, in the fifteen years since Tajikistan's unexpected independence following the collapse of the Soviet Union, the population had seen a great deal of change. Much of that change had been bad, including a collapsed economy, hyperinflation, high unemployment, and a murderous civil war. It was not difficult to see why many people might favour stability over more political change. And many were satisfied with a sham election that didn't risk rocking their fragile boat. It wasn't an attitude I would expect in Canada, and our OSCE mission's primary criticism of the election was the "marked absence of competition."[19] But in the particular context of Tajikistan, I could see how it made sense. Cynical Tajik friends told me they were sure the results were fixed, but ironically fixed to give Rahmonov a result lower than he really got, rather than higher, so that foreigners would have the impression of a more competitive race than actually took place.

Making sense of how competitive candidates were in a Ukrainian election was even more complicated.

II

"But why are there all these 'technical' candidates? If they haven't got a chance of winning, what are they running for?" There were eighteen candidates on the ballot in the 2010 elections for the president of Ukraine and most of them did not look like serious contenders. Our interpreter for that election, Pavlo, was waving his arms around in the front seat of the car with frustration at these numbers.

We were driving southwest out of the city of Kharkiv along a modern divided highway across the snow-covered steppes on a brisk December morning. We were on our way to visit election officials in the small town of Kupiansk who were preparing for the presidential vote. Road trips were always good occasions to see the country and talk about our work, in between and during my colleagues' frequent cigarette breaks.

"Well, that's part of our job," I said from the backseat where I sat with Vladimir, my Russian long-term observer partner. "We have to figure out why all those minor candidates are running. And we have only a few weeks left to understand it all!"

So-called technical candidates are a common feature of Ukrainian elections. A technical candidate has no intention of really participating in the campaign or winning any votes. Instead, they are usually running to control places on the commissions that implement the election.

I had never seen anything like this in Canada. In Canadian elections, each poll has a few hundred voters and is run by one deputy returning officer plus one poll clerk. In theory, the deputy returning officer and poll clerk represent different political parties. However, in practice, it is rare that Canadian parties can recommend many members prepared to work on polling day, so most election workers are interested citizens who don't represent any party. Deputy returning officers and poll clerks often don't meet until election day, and their partnership is over as soon as they finish counting and pack up their materials that evening.

Ukrainian polls are much larger. They serve a few thousand voters and are run by a commission made up of many members, all appointed by parties or candidates. Commissions have many meetings over several weeks and regularly vote on decisions. Multi-member commissions also run the elections at the district level in Ukraine. At the Canadian equivalent of the riding, only one returning officer is responsible for all key decisions.

In the 2010 Ukrainian presidential elections, each of the eighteen candidates on the ballot could nominate two representatives for each commission, so election commissions were bloated with a total of thirty-six members. However, it was rumoured that commission members who sat in the name of a technical candidate didn't really represent that candidate. Rather, they secretly – or not so secretly – represented another candidate or party, giving that party a larger say in commission decisions.

It can be a challenge to figure out which party the technical candidate is really supporting. Several of the presidential candidates in 2010 had virtually no visible campaign, so we wanted to test who they were really rooting for. At the District Election Commission in Kupiansk, I tried out a script I had developed for teasing out the true allegiance of election commission members who served in the name of suspect candidates. It played upon their legitimate pride in their extensive election experience.

"Have you worked on elections before?" I would ask innocently.

"Of course," was the typical answer. "I've been working on elections for years!"

"That's great. You have so much experience! So, I see you are representing candidate X this time?"

"Yes, I am" was the most common answer. Although sometimes the member would have to ask their colleagues which candidate they were supposed to be representing, which was a good indication in itself that they were not genuine supporters.

"I understand that candidate X didn't run in the last election," I would continue.

"No."

"So, may I ask which party you represented last time?"

At this point, commission members who were quick on the uptake would realize that this question was a setup and would conveniently find they had forgotten who they worked for during the last election. But many would just tell me the name of the party. And from that I would infer that they were probably representing that party again this time. If several commission members representing the same technical candidate had all worked for the same party on previous elections, it was pretty safe to assume that the technical candidate had been proposed by, or was working for, that same party to increase the number of representatives of that party on the election commission.

It was a gotcha moment that I didn't always feel comfortable with, but it allowed us to better understand the game that was being played with technical candidates. The commission members were not nefarious characters. They were mostly hardworking citizens who had been recruited – and were being paid a pittance – to fill a role in a bigger political game. They might never have to vote on a decision that would trigger their party allegiance anyway. But if the election results were close, and there were poll-level decisions to be made that would invalidate ballots, they knew when to raise their hands and when to keep them down.

Back in Kharkiv, we worked another tactic: asking the representatives of suspect candidates where their regional party headquarters was located. The answers were typically vague until a tired District Election Commission chair, Vera Demyanova (who officially represented the minor candidate, Mykhailo Brodskyy), finally broke down and admitted to us that the so-called headquarters for her candidate and for two other suspect candidates, Serhiy Ratushniak and Vasyl Protyvsikh, were all inside the headquarters of the locally dominant Party of Regions. That gave it all away. And indeed, for the second round of the election, Vera came out of the closet and represented the Party of Regions candidate, Yanukovich.

At the same time, it seemed likely to me that some technical candidates saw international observers as a tool in their game. They knew that observers look for visible campaign materials as evidence of a legitimate candidacy. One day, when I was walking my regular morning exercise route in central Kharkiv, I came across a new billboard for a technical candidate who had zero local profile. "Has he put that up just for me?" I wondered. "Is he expecting me to put that in our report?" And of course, I did – as an example of the exception that proved the rule that this candidate was not a serious contender.

By the time election day rolled around, we had drawn some conclusions. I assembled a tongue-in-cheek summary for the short-term observers about the diverse motives of eighteen candidates on the presidential ballot.

Viktor Yanukovich used to be the prime minister, and now he wants to be president. Yulia Tymoshenko is the prime minister, and now she wants to be president. Viktor Yushchenko is the president, but he would probably be happy just to be prime minister again.

Volodymyr Lytvyn is the speaker of the Parliament and looks pretty desperate just to hang on to that job. Arseniy Yatsenyuk used to be speaker of the Parliament and might be happy to take that job again.

Serhiy Tihipko is running for president, but really he wants to be prime minister now and maybe president later on. Anatoliy Hrytsenko used to be minister of defense, but now he is positioning his party for local government elections even though there is no army at that level.

Oleh Tyahnybok used to be a Socialist Nationalist, which isn't so far from a National Socialist, and might even be mistaken for a Nazi, and he certainly would like to see a "pure" Ukrainian in charge of the country.

Vasyl Protyvsikh – protyvsikh means "against all" in Ukrainian – changed his family name to run in the election on an anti-establishment ticket, but really he is supporting Yanukovich. Serhiy Ratushniak and Mykhailo Brodskyy are also non-partisan men who actually back Yanukovich's party.

Female candidates Inna Bohoslovska and Liudmyla Suprun are chasing the women's vote, but in the second round of the election they will hand their votes to the man – Yanukovich, not the woman – Tymoshenko.

Petro Symonenko used to be a communist, and in fact he still is a communist, only no one knows what that means anymore. Oleksandr Moroz used to be a communist, but now he is a socialist, which means he can move between camps more easily.

Yuri Kostenko is still a mystery and doesn't seem to have very much support, while Oleksandr Pabat and Oleh Riabokon don't seem to have any supporters at all.

In sum, I was beginning to see that a presidential election was about a lot more than choosing a president. It was really a broad political process involving a large amount of posturing and jockeying for position among a small number of rich and powerful people that would result in a new president and a probably a new prime minister, possibly a new speaker of the Parliament and quite likely snap elections for Parliament followed by scheduled local government elections. At the end of which an exhausted and disillusioned electorate would have a new government made up mostly of the same people, backed by the same oligarchs continuing along in their traditionally corrupt ways.

The fight against that corruption came to a head only a few years after this election, as patriotism and military bona fides gained new relevance for people who wanted to get nominated and win on the ballots in parliamentary elections in 2014.

III

Before we even set foot on the tarmac in the western Ukrainian region of Ivano-Frankivsk in 2014, just two words confirmed that there had been significant changes in Ukraine since the elections I had observed in 2010 and 2012. As our plane taxied along the runway towards the airport terminal, the pilot gave the usual spiel announcing our arrival, alerting us to the local weather and thanking us for flying his airline. Then, after a slight pause, he added, "*Slava Ukraini*." Glory to Ukraine. He seemed to be saying: and of course, I am onside with the revolution, as I assume are all of you. *Slava Ukraini* had become the rallying cry of the Euromaidan Revolution that had swept through Ukrainian politics just seven months earlier, resulting in a complete change of government and preparing a very unusual field for these early parliamentary elections that we had come to observe.

In 2010, I had watched the Party of Regions candidate Viktor Yanukovich win the presidency. He didn't have a large margin – he defeated Yulia Tymoshenko by only 3.5 per cent in the second-round run-off – but he was the legitimate winner of the election. However, the results of the vote showed that the country was nearly evenly divided between two contrasting views about future political and economic alignment. The Party of Regions promoted returning to the strong ties with Russia that had dominated much of Ukraine in the previous century, while Tymoshenko's party favoured stronger alignment with Europe. In the 2012 parliamentary elections, the Party of Regions won fewer votes than in previous rounds, but it was still a force to be reckoned with, taking 41 per cent of the seats in Parliament.

However, in the fall of 2013 the president and his party lost legitimacy in the eyes of many Ukrainians when he rejected a European Union-Ukraine Association Agreement in favour of closer economic ties with Russia. While I was working on research contracts at home in Canada, over the three months between November 2013 and February 2014, I often had a window open in the corner of my computer monitor, playing a live stream from the demonstrations that sprang up in Independence Square in Kyiv and in other cities across the country that became known as Euromaidan. Despite being thousands of kilometres away, I was able to watch in real time as Ukrainians rallied and fought in their central squares – the *maidan* – against what many saw as a step backwards towards closer ties with the Russian state. As the weeks wore on, the situation in Kyiv became increasingly chaotic and violent, and demonstrators were shot in the streets. Eventually, on 21 February 2014, Yanukovich abandoned his position as president and left the country, and the Party of Regions began to disintegrate. In Kyiv, the opposition took the opportunity to take over the presidency and Parliament. In the south and east, other forces saw a different opportunity.

On 28 February 2014, I was watching a live stream from a camera mounted on a utility pole outside the gates of a Ukrainian-held military base in the southern port city of Sevastopol, Crimea. In the foreground,

I could see unidentified soldiers pacing outside the gates, while far in the background I glimpsed what appeared to be Ukrainian soldiers on parade inside the base. After a while, a man below the camera looked up directly at me – and all the other people around the world monitoring the situation over the internet – and pointed the camera out to his colleagues. One of them disappeared from view below the camera, and the camera image began to vibrate. Suddenly, he appeared in close-up having scaled the pole to the height of the camera. The last image I saw before the Russians took over that base was a young Russian soldier's hand reaching out to shut down transmissions from that camera. I stared at the blank feed for a few moments, hoping it might be reconnected, but of course it wasn't. This chilling moment was confirmed later that day by the news that Russia had taken control of Crimea from Ukraine.

Almost immediately a violent insurgency broke out in the eastern regions of Donetsk and Luhansk. On 13 April 2014 the Ukrainian government launched the Anti-Terrorist Operation – which came to be referred to as the ATO – to attempt to regain control of the eastern regions. Unfortunately, the Ukrainian army in 2014 turned out to be weak, disorganized, and unprepared for the conflict. Drawing on the spirit of self-organization that had driven the demonstrations across the country, multiple volunteer battalions – non-government militias by any other name – mobilized to take up the slack left by the army and defend the Ukrainian cause. Fighting continued through the summer. An agreement for a ceasefire had been brokered on 5 September 2012 in Minsk, Belarus, a few weeks before my Finish partner Pekka and I arrived to join the OSCE mission monitoring early parliamentary elections at the end of September. But the fighting had not really stopped, and there would be no voting in parts of the country that were still outside government control.

Our job as election observers did not officially include monitoring the conflict. Nevertheless, the war was constantly in the background (and sometimes in the foreground) of the 2014 campaign. During our security briefing in Kyiv the core team listed thirty-nine volunteer battalions, each reporting between 100 and 500 members. Some were nominally subordinate to the Ministry of Defense while others theoretically reported to the Ministry of Interior. By 2015 most of these battalions would be brought fully under government control, but in the fall of 2014 many were still operating independently. These battalions and their supporters were passionate Ukrainian nationalists, but many remained skeptical of the Ukrainian state.[20] At the same time, some battalions were aligned with political parties contesting the elections and were angling for direct representation in Parliament. Members of the army were also candidates in some constituencies. So we were definitely interested in observing their activities in the political field.

Despite being 600 kilometres southwest of Kyiv, and more than 1,000 kilometres west of the war zone, the revolution and conflict were very immediate for many people in Ivano-Frankivsk. Walking through the central city park, I found a line of poignant memorials, huge piles of floral wreaths, bouquets, and candles surrounding photographs of local men who had died in the fight.

The first and biggest mound of flowers was for Roman Gurik, a nineteen-year-old philosophy student from the university in Ivano-Frankivsk, who was shot by a sniper on 19 February 2014 while demonstrating in Kyiv. Roman's serious young face, with his unruly student haircut, had become famous across the country as the youngest martyr among the Heavenly Hundred demonstrators who were killed in Kyiv in January and February. His photo, which was probably taken for an ID card or passport, showed the classic face of a hero with even features and a flawless completion looking straight at the viewer with a calm expression that seemed to combine innocence with determination. He couldn't have had any idea what role his activism would play when that photo was taken, but in death his image had become a potent symbol for the revolution.[21] We saw those dark eyes staring coolly at us from memorial displays of photos of the hundred martyrs at nearly every government building we visited during the 2014 election. For the people of Ivano-Frankivsk, the conflict at hand wasn't an abstract debate over policy options; it was a personal fight that their family and neighbours were directly engaged in.

The first weekend, as I explored the city, I came across a fundraiser for one of the self-defence battalions in a city square. Members of the public were making donations for the privilege of being photographed holding weapons. A woman in a dress coat and leather boots cheerfully brandished a military rifle while her partner took snaps. A man in camouflage helped outfit the next person in line, a young girl in an orange hoodie and floral pants. First, he put a soldier's helmet on her head. Then, he propped the empty casing of a rocket-propelled grenade launcher on her shoulder so her mother could take her picture as a future warrior. Elsewhere, I saw passers-by showing their patriotism by tying strips of fabric onto a camouflage net. In the supermarket where I shopped for groceries, there was a cart at the checkout collecting food donations for the volunteers in the ATO. We learned later that prior to working for us, our driver had been using his personal vehicle to make runs across the country to deliver food, supplies, and men to the volunteer battalions on the front lines in the east.

With so much attention on the conflict in the east, it was no surprise that many of the candidates in this 2014 election strove to be identified as combatants. Several candidates appeared in their campaign materials dressed in camouflage, capitalizing on their bona fides as participants in the ATO. One with a very visible campaign in the Ivano-Frankivsk region was Yuri Tymoshenko, a local fifty-three-year-old activist who had joined the demonstrations in Kyiv and then volunteered for the National Guard when the fighting broke out. We saw him on billboards around the region, posing in military garb and holding an automatic rifle beside a road sign for Sloviansk in the Donetsk region, where a major battle had taken place in June that liberated the town from separatist control. The khaki look worked for Yuri, who beat all the competition in his constituency, including two other candidates in uniform. He went on to sit in Parliament with the People's Front, aligned with Prime Minister Arseniy Yatsenyuk. (Interestingly, in 2019, Yulia Tymoshenko accused Yuri Tymoshenko of being a technical candidate when he ran for president. Yulia alleged that his very similar name was only on the ballot to confuse voters.[22])

IV

In 2015, a year and a half after the conflict began, Ukrainian forces are mostly united, but there is no resolution to the conflict in sight. Appeals to patriotism still have strong currency in Kirovohrad, but how that patriotism is defined varies. Several of the parties with western Ukrainian roots define patriotism in terms of military service in the ATO. Half of the candidates chosen by the right-wing nationalist Freedom Party are on active service and all of them are dressed in camouflage on their posters. Like the Freedom Party, many candidates for the new UKROP Party are also in military service, and like the Self Reliance Party, they are proud to have no connection with previous governments. In contrast, candidates for the Opposition Bloc, which has become a home for many people who served in previous Party of Regions administrations, talk about patriotism in terms of supporting local business through buying local and subsidizing local production. The war is not a central issue in the local government elections, but it is there in the background of the campaign nevertheless.

4 Win the Votes · Round One

Prepare the field Win the votes Buy the votes Steal the votes Invalidate the votes

4.1 Following the Campaign

The heart of any election is the campaign when parties and candidates reach out to voters to win their trust and confidence and secure their vote on election day. Political campaigns usually employ direct outreach through advertising, handouts, rallies, and meeting with individual voters, in addition to indirect outreach through the media. As election observers, we are always watching to see if there is genuine competition in the campaign and a level playing field for all candidates and parties on the ground and in the media. We are also on the lookout for any interference or barriers that could prevent some candidates from campaigning, and any violence or intimidation against candidates or voters. We also monitor whether campaign finance laws are followed and if there is misuse of public resources that can give incumbents an unfair advantage.[1] We have to find practical ways to track all of this as we begin to follow the 2015 campaign in Kirovohrad.

"There's another Opposition Bloc billboard," our driver Anton points out as we pull up to an intersection.

"Right!" I say, as I put a tick next to Opposition Bloc on my checklist.

As we drive around Kirovohrad in the first weeks to meet with party representatives and candidates, I carry around a checklist in a folder to tally the campaign materials we see on the streets. It is a bit like a playing a license plate game on a summer vacation drive, keeping track of which parties and candidates have a visible campaign. When I go for lunch at one of the cafés near the central square, I note the campaign tents pitched there and pick up any new materials on offer. Techniques like these don't produce a scientific sample of campaign activity, but at least I have an accurate record of what we have seen when it comes time to write up our weekly report.

On election day, voters in Kirovohrad city will cast ballots for regional council, district council, and city district council. It is a complicated election for candidates and voters. Some council seats are majority races and other council members will be elected on a proportional representation system from lists of candidates prepared by the parties. Voters will also cast a ballot directly for the mayor. The mayor needs an absolute majority to win the race, and if no candidate gets a majority in the first round, there will be a second-round run-off between the top two candidates.

Over four elections in Ukraine, I have seen a fairly consistent style of campaigning, some of which is different from what we see in Canada. In our first week in Kirovohrad I count seven national parties advertising with campaign billboards along the highways and posters in the light-box advertising panels along city streets and on bus shelters. Election campaigns are very good business for the companies that own those assets! And there are branded tents, staffed by campaign workers in coloured pinnies handing out free brochures and newspapers about their candidates to passers-by in the city streets. One thing I have not seen in Ukrainian elections are lawn signs. Unlike Canadians and Americans, many of whom are happy to show their neighbours which party they support, most Ukrainian voters are circumspect about their political choices.

Probably the most common campaign handouts are the calendar cards, glossy wallet-sized cards with the candidate's name and photo on one side and a calendar on the reverse. I suppose the parties hope that voters will keep the card handy in their pocket up to election day to remind them who to vote for. For me they are too much like hockey cards, and irresistible to collect. I post my growing collection on the office wall to help track some of the many candidates we observe. In fact, I suspect that most election observers have a collection of party swag they have collected on their missions: T-shirts, desk flags, music CDs, key chains,

Christmas tree decorations, and pencils and pens, etc. A neutral observer wouldn't display any of this swag while on the mission, but a lot comes back in the suitcase to add to the clutter in the home office.

II

Unlike in Canada, where party politics play little role in municipal elections, national political parties are very active in local politics in Ukraine. However, political parties in Ukraine are less ideological than Canadian parties and cannot easily be placed on a left-right axis. Many would characterize the big Ukrainian parties that have strong ties to oligarchs as more akin to lobbyists for financial, industrial, and regional clans than western-style political parties.[2] Moreover, Ukrainian politics are dominated by personalities. Indeed, party names have often reflected the leader rather than any ideological leanings, such as the Bloc Petro Poroshenko Solidarnist (BPPS), the Bloc Yulia Tymoshenko, and the Radical Party of Oleh Lyashko.

Perhaps hoping to draw irrelevant comparisons with American politics, foreign analysts often attribute a simplistic two-party red-blue divide to the Ukrainian political scene, but this metaphor will not explain the diversity of candidates in this election. The results of elections like the 2010 run-off that I observed between Yanukovich (whose Party of Regions used blue) and Tymoshenko (whose Fatherland Party used red) did show the country divided diagonally in half, southwest to northeast. The majority of voters northwest of the line voted red for Tymoshenko and her more European-aligned vision, while the majority in regions southeast of the line voted blue for Yanukovich and his Russian-leaning vision. However, that line ran right through the middle of the Kirovohrad region, where the region's population was fairly evenly divided. As it is, run-off elections obscure the fact that Ukraine is not a two-party state, and there are many parties and colours active in politics.

There are 866 positions as councillors or mayors up for grabs across the region in these local elections and a total of 5,015 candidates across all the ballots. Four national parties are fielding enough candidates to gain or maintain their foothold in the region. The two biggest are the Fatherland Party with 854 candidates and the BPPS with 814 running for office. The Opposition Bloc with 628 and the Radical Party of Oleh Lyashko with 567 candidates are not far behind.

Arguably, the party to beat during these local elections is the BPPS, as it is the biggest red party running nationally. Up to now, my only interest in Petro Poroshenko has been driven by my sweet tooth. Poroshenko is known as the chocolate king because much of his massive wealth comes from the confectionery business. I was introduced to the delights of Ukrainian chocolate from my first days in the country in 2001 when I discovered that even in the depths of economic collapse you could still buy top-notch local chocolate and champagne in Odesa. Since then, I have often walked past – and into – Poroshenko's flagship Roshen chocolate store on Khreschatyk Street, Kyiv's central promenade not far from the President Hotel. The store windows glow brightly in the night and a clockwork roller coaster for candy in the front window brings to mind magical images from Charlie and the Chocolate Factory. The shop is every child's fantasy with bins of individual foil-wrapped chocolates and artistically stacked pyramids of packaged treats.

Poroshenko was elected president in May 2014 after Yanukovich was driven from office in February. BPPS was formed in August 2014 through a merger between Poroshenko's Solidarnist Party and Vitali Klitchko's UDAR Party, and as the presidential party they have access to both administrative resources and media. When he ran for president, Poroshenko promised to divest himself of his business interests, in particular his chocolate factory in Russia, but that has not happened, which is eroding his credibility.[3] He also has not divested himself from his national TV channel 5, and he has close relations with the oligarch behind Inter, another national TV channel. No one expects those channels to have anything but good to say about him and his BPPS candidates.

Like BPPS, the Fatherland Party is fielding a nearly full slate of candidates across Kirovohrad region. The Fatherland Party is led by Yulia Tymoshenko, who was first elected to Parliament from a constituency in this region nearly two decades ago. Her distinct image as a Ukrainian nationalist politician had been strategically cultivated. In the early 2000s, she took to wearing her brown hair bleached blond and wrapped around her head in a peasant-style braid, cleverly combining this rural Ukrainian hairstyle with a wardrobe of conservative but expensive designer dresses. While Tymoshenko is Ukraine's most successful woman politician who narrowly lost a run for the presidency in 2010, she is indelibly associated with disappointment in my mind. I remember a bitterly cold winter evening in December 2009, when I waited for more than an hour in the snow in Rosa Luxemburg Square in Kharkiv as Tina Carol, one of Ukraine's most famous women singers, performed in a concert on behalf of Tymoshenko. Carol and her backup singers sang and danced on the big stage wrapped in classy fur coats, hats, and mitts, and her elegant pop tunes echoed off the walls of the buildings around the square. But Tymoshenko herself never showed up. The music was great, but we didn't learn anything about the candidate or her program. Her plane had been turned back due to the snow and we went home with frozen feet and a cold attitude. A few weeks later I tuned in for the round two presidential TV debate. In this case it was Tymoshenko's opponent Yanukovich who didn't show up. However, Tymoshenko wasn't going to let the airtime go to waste, and she droned on for more than an hour – very dull listening. In 2012, we drove past her family home in Dnipropetrovsk, but she was nowhere to be seen as the Yanukovich regime had removed her from the political competition by jailing her on corruption charges.

By the time I did finally see Tymoshenko in person in 2014, she had lost a lot of the momentum she had in 2010. But in a country that loves a victim, Tymoshenko was making the most of the martyr's reputation she had earned over three years in jail. She had been released in February during the Euromaidan protests and, undeterred by her incarceration, she went straight from jail to the stage in the Kyiv *maidan* to address the crowds from a wheelchair. She came second in the May 2014 presidential elections, with only 12 per cent of the vote. In October, we watched her deliver a standard stump speech in the central square in Kolomyia. The crowd of her devoted supporters, many of them women of her age – she was then in her fifties – showed a lot of sympathy for her as a woman struggling to make her way in the man's world of Ukrainian politics. In 2015 she is still in the game, and with a full slate of candidates across our region the Fatherland Party is not a spent force.

The party that really is a spent force is the Party of Regions, which has gone from being the dominant party in 2012 to being disgraced during the Euromaidan Revolution, and then effectively disintegrating over 2014. However, in practice Ukrainian politicians are often opportunistic and many have changed parties over the years, while many parties have split and/or merged into coalitions, "factions," and "blocs." The collapse of the Party of Regions has not meant that all its party members have retired from politics or that its Russian-leaning ideology has disappeared. Local media in Kirovohrad are tracking former Party of Regions members running for Kirovohrad city council seats for six different parties. Most prominent is the new blue Opposition Bloc that has emerged from the ashes of the Party of Regions like a phoenix and – so there will be no doubt about its roots – has taken on the familiar blue colour. We see that blue colour still painted on park infrastructure in Kirovohrad in 2015, a subtle reminder of the staying power of this political force, despite the demise of the original party.

III

"Here we are, out in the middle of nowhere, and there's another Party of Regions blue play structure!" We were looking for the poll in a small rural village near the city of Dnipropetrovsk on a 2012 fall day.

"Oh, oh, oh. Wait, I have to write that down." Kateryna was digging in her bag.

"What?"

"'The middle of nowhere.' I've never heard that phrase before, but I can tell exactly what it means. I love it!" She immediately wrote it down in the notebook where she was collecting useful phrases. I was constantly impressed with our interpreter's commitment to improving her already excellent English vocabulary whenever she could. If only I had collected more useful Russian phrases, I would have been a lot further ahead in my language acquisition than I was.

We were out in the field visiting rural polls around Dnipropetrovsk, when we came across yet another new blue playground structure in the village of Rudka. Like all the others we had seen, it was painted Party of Regions blue and bore the party logo and best wishes "to the little residents of Rudka" from the governor and the local member of Parliament who was running for re-election. The kids wouldn't care who was credited, but their parents might well be grateful. There was no way to be sure, but I thought it highly unlikely that the party actually paid for all these pieces of municipal infrastructure. More likely, despite the Party of Regions branding, the funds came from the regional government budget currently under the control of the Party of Regions. That suggested it was a prime example of the misuse of administrative resources to promote the party in power during the current parliamentary elections. But, with the long game in mind, the sturdy blue swings were also there to build the party brand for future contests as well.

IV

In Kirovohrad, Matti and I find that for many political parties these 2015 local elections are part of their preparations for parliamentary elections. When we head out with Oksana in the first weeks to meet representatives of the parties fielding significant numbers of candidates like the Fatherland, Opposition Bloc, and the Radical Parties, they stress that their goal in local government is to build their base to achieve national power. They seem to see local government as primarily a means to achieve power in Kyiv for their party, rather than a tool for delivering services to the local population. However, these parties are not pushing a distinct national or local platform. I am surprised that very few of these party representatives identify municipal issues as important local issues, and almost none seem to focus on the actual powers and responsibilities of local councils. When we ask, most can identify roads and utilities as local issues, but no one speaks about local schools or hospitals or parks, and no one names a specific road that they will repair or can explain how they will deal with the rising costs of utilities or other issues that municipal governments in Canada regularly deal with. We wonder if the candidates for mayor will have a clearer vision for addressing the needs of local voters.

4.2 Through the Eyes of the Media

I

Whether or not I am observing an election, when I arrive in a new country I want to browse the local media to find out what are the hot button issues of the moment. An election observer monitors media during an election to understand whether candidates' campaigns are getting fair and balanced coverage in the media, to assess the tone of the media coverage, and most importantly to understand whether the media offers local voters enough "diverse, comprehensive, and impartial information" to make an informed choice about who to vote for.

Observers consider both the advertising that candidates and parties pay to have placed in media, and any more objective coverage of the campaign by independent news sources – should such a thing exist in the country. Ideally, we would examine print media (newspaper and magazines), broadcast media (TV and radio), and online sources (news sites and social media). But, given the limited time and human resources, we can only look at a small sample of the information available to the voter.

The years that I have been observing elections in Ukraine have been a period of great change in how politicians and voters around the world exchange information through media. The OSCE methodology has had a hard time keeping up and the mission budget always limits how many people can be assigned to media and what they can observe. The missions I served on typically had one media analyst assigned at the national level, who would have one dedicated assistant and an additional team of local media monitors who took on the time-consuming tasks like watching national TV coverage. It was a necessary part of the long-term observer's job to complement the national media monitoring at the local level.

In the 2020s we can access built-in translation for most online media and most print media is also available online. Twenty years ago, if you couldn't read the local language, the picture you got from the media in a new country could be limited to the international press or the odd English-language paper printed in the capital. When I first lived in Ukraine in 2001, the small weekly *Kyiv Post* was the only English-language paper in the country, and *The Economist* was the only English magazine I could find in the whole city of Odesa. If I wanted to access online news I had to descend into a local internet cafe, a dark and eye-wateringly smoky basement dominated by pre-teen boys playing networked games of Counter Strike and shouting at each other over the monitors as they chain-smoked and shot at phantom terrorists. The desire for better access to local news was a strong motivation behind my drive to study the Russian language.

By the time I took on my first Ukrainian long-term observer assignment in 2009, I could read a fair bit of Russian, albeit slowly, and I had early Russian-English translation software loaded on my computer. It certainly helped that my long-term observer partner on that first mission, Vladimir, was a Russian diplomat who could take on a lot of our media monitoring. That was not the case on my other missions, and we relied heavily on our interpreters to help analyze the print and TV coverage. We also tried to talk directly with some journalists to get some sense of the independence of the media and the objectivity of their output.

II

When we met Vasyl Voevodko, deputy editor of the *Voice of Pokuttja*, in 2014, in the office of his district-government-owned newspaper in Sniaytyn, in the Ivano-Frankivsk region of western Ukraine, he was surprisingly frank about how the media operated during elections.

"I'd say elections are the good season for my journalists!" Vasyl told us. "They have to set aside their regular journalism, of course. But they can earn some good money by producing articles for the candidates and parties."

He went on to explain to my Finish long-term observer partner Pekka and me how his local paper, with a circulation of 2,000, approached the political campaign: "Our budget from local government is small, and we don't get much advertising revenue, so we can't pay our journalists a big salary. So, it's great that they can get some extra income during an election."

"Are you saying that all the articles about the campaign in your paper have been paid for by a candidate or party?" Pekka confirmed.

"Certainly. We will print articles from any of the candidates or parties."

We flipped through the paper and we could see articles for all the major parties and some independent candidates, so the campaign was getting wide coverage. The only problem – from our perspective anyway – was that none of the articles indicated that they were effectively paid advertisements.

"And what are the important issues in this campaign at the local level?" I asked.

He pondered a moment. "I would say the important issues in this campaign are really all national: Ukrainian independence, the war in the Donbas, pressure from Russia … and of course, corruption."

We had to leave it at that. But Pekka and I agreed later that it was ironic that he was concerned about corruption, but he didn't consider printing articles paid for by candidates in the guise of independent reporting as a problem. This was a common practice in traditional Ukrainian media, and it was never clear to me whether the Ukrainian reader actually imagined this kind of reporting was objective, or whether they just assumed that all the campaign coverage would be slanted in favour of the subject, and took it all with a grain of salt. Certainly, research suggests that most Ukrainians are sceptical about the news media and suspect that coverage usually reflects the bias of the owner/producer whether that is government, oligarchs, and/or whoever directly paid for the article.[4] Those suspicions extended to the major TV channels, all of which are controlled by oligarchs who are not shy about promoting their business interests, and the local state channels that were controlled by local government. However, social media had already begun to undermine the ability of those powers to control the message.

III

Ironically, it was watching TV during the 2012 parliamentary elections in Dnipropetrovsk that the rising power of social media really hit home for me. After an hour of trying to follow a TV comedy show in Russian, my brain was exhausted and I had zoned out. But I suddenly recognized that subject of this last sketch of the *Vecherini Kvartal* special on national TV was actually someone I had met the previous week. I sat up on the edge of my sofa and leaned forward. The diminutive leader of the *Kvartal 95* comedy troupe, Volodymyr Zelensky, was impersonating a popular talk show host, bouncing around the stage and challenging one of the other comedians to tell his story. The comedic story he told was built around a satirical meme that had spun off far and wide on social media about being punished for voting for the ruling party. But the original story had started in a small community outside the city of Dnipropetrovsk, where we were observing these parliamentary elections.[5]

I had been introduced to Zelensky and the *Kvartal 95* comedy team during my first week of election observation in Ukraine in 2009. Our interpreter recommended we watch the show that evening because *Kvartal 95* was the most famous comedy troupe in the country, and much of their humour revolved around politics. I could immediately see that they were similar to Canada's *22 Minutes* troupe, and Zelensky had a lot in common with Rick Mercer. I couldn't follow much of the language at that time, as their Russian was quick and there were many linguistic jokes that played on the audience's bilingualism in Ukrainian and Russian. But it was obvious which politicians they were skewering.

I was immediately drawn to the thirty-one-year-old Zelensky. He derived a lot of his laughs from the contrast between his small stature and his deep voice, as he talked up at his much taller colleagues while they were forced to look down at him. He had an expressive face and an energetic, even frenetic, stage presence that kept him at the centre of attention even in group sketches. I also appreciated how he enunciated clearly, so that I caught a lot more of what he said in Russian than some of the others. And when he talked directly to the crowd, he achieved an impressive intimacy with the audience in the large auditorium and across the airwaves. I made sure to tune in for *Kvartal 95* specials during every election I covered in Ukraine.

The story behind the *Kvartal 95* sketch that caught my attention in 2012 started with a form of traditional media used extensively in Ukrainian political campaigns – a billboard displayed near Dnipropetrovsk. A young local politician, Maxim Golosny, wanted to protest the ruling party's lack of action on infrastructure in his rural community. So, in the run up to the parliamentary elections he had paid for a billboard with an image of a Ukrainian grandmother in a floral head scarf with her cat, accompanied by the slogan, "When I heard my grandson voted for the Party of Regions, I transferred the house to the cat." It was a slap in the face for the ruling party and the billboard was only up for three days before the authorities had it removed. But in a telling example of how political protest was being transformed by new media, the image took on a life of its own as an internet meme and circulated widely in Ukraine and even outside the country.

When Golosny found out that international observers were covering his district, he wanted to tell us his story.[6] He suggested that my Dutch long-term observer partner Bart and I meet him in a coffee shop on the central square opposite the Dnipropetrovsk Opera Ballet Theatre. Golosny was an intense young man, and he furrowed his eyebrows as he gave us a passionate account of his novel – if a bit naive – story. He claimed that as a result of his billboard protest he was under pressure from the ruling party and had gone into hiding and moved his wife and child to a secret location. Unnamed sources had told him he was at risk of arrest, and he feared he would be taken in after the election. However, as he chose to meet us in a central café, and was just back from a presentation to a group of students in Ternopil, we thought his actions didn't quite line up with his words. But, perhaps his real goal was to publicly demonstrate that he was on the radar of international observers as insurance against further harassment.

Nevertheless, the speed with which his billboard came down showed that the local powers were not prepared to tolerate public satire in traditional media like a billboard. However, they probably had not understood how difficult it was to restrain a compelling image in the age of social media. Sitting in front of my TV that evening, I could see that the online image had become so famous that it had come full circle and become fodder for Zelensky's comedy on the traditional media platform of television, and national media at that. In the future we observers would have to follow these stories in all the different media as best we could.

IV

In 2015, the OSCE is only monitoring traditional media like newspapers and TV at the national level. One of the first things Matti and I do when we start our work in Kirovohrad is to send our driver Anton out to buy one of every newspaper on the newsstand so that we can begin analyzing how the local elections are being covered in the local print media.

However, this is the first election where I also follow local politics in our region extensively through online news sites and social networking sites such as Facebook,[7] although we don't have a formal methodology. Our core team analysts tell us that social media has the potential to provide an alternative viewpoint to traditional media and we are vaguely advised that it might be useful to follow local election stakeholders on Facebook, but that is about it. In fact, I have never thought of Facebook as a research tool before. I quickly learn its value.

The truth is, I have been a holdout on the smart phone front and am still using a 2G phone in Canada in 2015. So, with a late-model 3G Android smart phone from the OSCE suddenly in hand, I have to get up to speed quickly. Fortunately, Oksana is an avid Facebook user, and she gives me lots of tips on the mobile app during our first days together. She explains how before the invasion of Crimea by the Russians in 2014, many Ukrainians relied on the Russian-owned social networks vкontakte and Odnoklasniki. But now, increasingly concerned about Russian interference in Ukrainian politics, she says many of her friends have rejected Russian social media and moved over to American-owned Facebook, which has become the dominant platform in Ukraine.

I have a Facebook account, but I rarely use it. I had set it up to connect with my nieces and nephews a few years earlier. But, as an in-joke with the kids, the account is in the name of a stuffed toy named Mr Racoon. When we start searching for and following local candidates and their managers on Facebook, the challenge is to see if the political actors will accept a friend request from a Canadian stuffed animal. Surprisingly, most do!

Luckily for us, most of these new Facebook users seem to have a weak grasp on privacy settings, leaving their personal pages public, which works well for us as we seek information and try to gauge the tenor of the campaign. And social media opens a fascinating window into the lives of local people outside of politics. Random personal moments may be revealed when you click through to the home page of someone who has commented on a candidate's post, turning them from an anonymous blowhard into a down-to-earth human who attends birthday parties and raises a glass with friends.

I connect with a number of candidates on Facebook, although I am challenged to read their posts, as Facebook is a few months away from rolling out translation on individual posts. However, as Facebook recognizes that I am connecting from Kirovohrad IP addresses, it begins to show me local campaign advertising. I also start reading local online news sites through Google Translate, and I bookmark the YouTube channels of key candidates and parties. All this allows for efficient use of our time, as Oksana and I scan social media while we wait for meetings to start, and I read online news in the quiet evenings in my apartment.

Eventually, I discover that the local state TV station regularly posts their talk shows on YouTube. One evening towards the end of the campaign I analyze a month's worth of broadcasts. By sliding my mouse along the timeline at the bottom of the YouTube window and watching the faces in the pop-up, I can easily calculate how much airtime each individual candidate has been allowed. This is a huge advance over earlier elections when we sometimes were asked to record TV election coverage on a VCR and then an assistant in the capital had tediously analyzed our stack of tapes with a stopwatch. My analysis in Kirovohrad shows that the local state TV station is clearly biased towards the leading red candidate, Andriy Raikovich. However, few people watch the channel so we doubt local TV coverage alone will impact the results. To understand more about the real impact of their campaigns we need to actually meet some candidates.

4.3 The Minor Candidates

I

One of the privileges of being an observer is that you get to meet the real people in front of the campaigns. However, tracking down and booking multiple candidates can be time consuming and difficult so we grab spontaneous meetings when they come up. The eight major parties that are widely represented across the region in these local elections are each fielding from 200 to 850 candidates for councils at the regional, district, city, and village levels. Four smaller parties have between 100 and 200 candidates each and nine other small parties have candidates in some of the races. We can't begin to meet all these candidates and parties, so in our third week of observations we focus in on the candidates running for city mayor.

Voters in the city of Kirovohrad will chose one of fourteen names on the ballot for mayor. There is no incumbent in this race. The last elected mayor resigned after the Euromaidan Revolution in 2014 and the man appointed to replace him is not running either. There is a big range in age and experience among the thirteen men and one woman who are on the ballot for mayor. Eight candidates, in their thirties, represent the post-Soviet generation who grew up after the collapse of the Soviet Union and independence of Ukraine in 1991. Three candidates, in their forties, had a communist childhood and came of age during the economic collapse and turbulence of the 1990s. Only three candidates are around sixty years old, old enough to have spent the formative first decade of their careers under Soviet rule in a planned economy. We want to understand how many of these candidates offer the genuine choice voters deserve in a well-functioning democracy.

"Hey Oksana," I nudge my interpreter with my elbow. "Isn't that Maksiuta?" The young man with the cleft chin and striking blue eyes nursing his coffee at a table by the window of the café looks too much like his election portraits to be mistaken. I turn to Matti who is managing our coffee order. "Shall we try and get an interview with him right now?"

"Why not?" I go over with Oksana to introduce ourselves and see if he will talk. Maksiuta agrees to join us when he has finished his coffee and we head upstairs to find a quiet table.

Andriy Maksiuta is one of the youngest at thirty-two. He tells us he had won his first election at eighteen and sat on an urban district council for four years a decade earlier. He is now involved with the anti-corruption movement. Although he had worked for Oleh Lyashko's Radical Party during the 2014 parliamentary elections, in this run for the mayor's office he has no party backing and nominated himself. Maksiuta seems to be a sincere young guy, and unlike the party representatives we had talked with, he has a strong focus on local issues such as municipal garbage, stray dogs, streetlights, and the water utility.

Before we bumped into Maksiuta that morning we had already met another mayoral candidate. Forty-nine-year-old Sergei Mikhalonok told us that ten years before he had been an active local leader with the Fatherland Party and won a seat on the city council. But in 2013, he had been swept up the Kirovohrad Euromaidan demonstrations and was now committed to systemic change. He had lost a self-nominated bid for a parliamentary seat in 2014, getting less than 3 per cent of the vote, but for this election he has the backing of the People's Control Party as their candidate for mayor. Mikhalonok also heads their party's list for seats on the city council, so we expect he has a better chance than Maksiuta at playing some role in local government in the future.

A couple of days later we meet the only woman running for mayor, thirty-nine-year-old Vita Atamanchuk. She has taken time off from her day job as a deputy head of the regional government administration to run, and she considers herself a pioneering women's activist diving into mayoral politics. This is her first time as a candidate, and she has tried but failed to get a nomination from the western Ukrainian-based Self Reliance Party. She thinks there are better opportunities for more women to enter politics now that so many men were fighting in the ATO. I think this is an odd spin to put on the war, but we are not there for a discussion, just to listen, so I keep my thoughts to myself. Atamanchuk doesn't seem to be a serious contender in this race, but perhaps she has visions of launching a longer career in politics. After all, Yulia Tymoshenko started her political career representing a constituency from the Kirovohrad region in the National Parliament in 1996.

We go across town from our meeting with Atamanchuk to meet a more competitive candidate, thirty-seven-year-old Andrei Tabalov. Tabalov has been nominated by Our Hometown Party for mayor, and also heads the party's list for city council. He studied in England and conducts our interview in English, which is a first for me in Ukraine. His father is a prominent local politician and businessman with profitable holdings in food processing and his uncle was deputy mayor in the past. Money doesn't seem to be a problem for Tabalov, and he tells us he will spend at least one million hryvnia (around $100,000 Canadian) on a high visibility campaign.

Afterwards, Oksana explains that Tabalov probably wants to revive his political career after a debacle in National Parliament. After serving on regional council, he had been elected along with his father to Parliament in 2012 representing the People's Front as part of the Fatherland opposition faction. However, in a scandal which was followed closely in Kirovohrad, father and son were unceremoniously turfed out of Parliament in a public brawl after being accused of crossing the floor to the Party of Regions. He ran as an independent in the 2014 parliamentary elections but got just 1,300 votes. Tabalov was charming and sophisticated with us, but Oksana tells us there are allegations he is involved in vote buying.

Another day, Andrei Leybenko joins us for coffee in Matti's hotel restaurant. One of the youngest candidates at thirty-two, he comes across as the most youthful and inexperienced. It looks like he had been nominated for mayor by the Opposition Bloc as a place holder, and he is also on the party lists for both regional and city council. His main claim to fame is that he is the manager of a popular regional hotline that was established by the local blue member of Parliament, Larin. Leybenko is the only candidate who admits to us that he has no illusions about the mayoral race and really seems to be hoping to just get onto city council.

Leybenko is sympathetic and generous and takes advantage of our meeting to introduce us to three young party workers, two women and a man, who have been threatened and traumatized on two occasions by thugs who insisted they take down their blue campaign tent. We listen to their story carefully and they are convincing in their description of what happened and how they felt about it. All we can do is report the incident to our core team. It is always unsettling to hear that young people are being harassed, whatever their political stripes, so I hope we at least provide moral support by taking their experience seriously.

After meeting Leybenko, we drive out to meet Anna Nizhnikova. Nizhnikova is not running for mayor, but she is the head of the Opposition Bloc Party organization in the city and the only woman to head a party list for city council. Thirty-nine-year-old Nizhnikova is the director of a prominent municipally-owned School for the Arts, and the artistic director and choreographer of a local competitive dance troupe. She immediately strikes me as a woman used to leading and being followed. It looks to me like she brings the steely discipline and determination of a professional dancer to everything she takes on, and she demonstrates a principal's efficient attitude during our interview. We feel a little bit like students who have been sent to the principal's office as various people come in and are quickly dispatched with curt instructions.

Nizhnikova admits that she was previously a member of the disgraced and defunct Party of Regions, which helps explain why she feels that local politicians should not have to be aligned with political parties. However, she says she is not ashamed of her previous allegiance. She is pragmatic. She doesn't completely agree with the Opposition Bloc position, but she feels she needs to be on the inside to effect change. She certainly likes the party strategy to put forward strong women candidates, a strategy we have not seen with other parties. She expresses pride in her fellow woman candidates who are featured on Opposition Bloc billboards around town, many of whom are school directors from top schools and one the head of the teachers' union. For her, they represent the face of competent and successful professional women. Nizhnikova is focusing her campaign on issues around education, culture, and health care, which is quite a contrast with the male candidates we have met who mainly talked about infrastructure, water supply, garbage, and animal shelters. Nizhnikova is a convincing, dynamic, and experienced leader, and we have to wonder why the young Leybenko, rather than her, has been selected to be the Opposition Bloc's candidate for mayor.

4.4 The Nationalist Candidates

I

There are two other minor candidates on the mayor's ballot who we want to keep an eye on. The role of radical right-wing nationalist parties in Ukrainian politics has attracted a lot of attention in the international media, not the least of which has been the Russian media. What I had seen on the ground was a much smaller movement than the media coverage might lead you to believe. Election results consistently showed that these parties had very minor support compared with the mainstream parties. However, both the Freedom Party and Oleh Lyashko's Radical

Party have nominated candidates for mayor, and we need to how they are reaching out to voters. I have been observing right-wing nationalist candidates since my first Ukrainian election in 2010.

"Can you translate this for me?" I handed the leaflet to the young woman from Kharkiv, who I was interviewing for an interpreter's job with a short-term observer team during the 2010 presidential elections. She took the paper and started reading. In this predominantly Russian-speaking city, I mainly needed to know how well the interpreters could interpret from Russian to English and back, but I also needed to know if they could translate Ukrainian. At the same time, I was curious whether they were familiar with some of the western Ukrainian parties and the candidates they were running for president.

The young woman's brows became increasingly furrowed as she read down the page and started to read it back to me in English. Finally, she stopped and asked, "What is this?!"

"That's a brochure we got from the Freedom Party. Oleh Tyahnybok's party. Do you know anything about them?"

"No! I've never seen this stuff." She was holding the paper out from her body like it was somehow contaminated. She was clearly uncomfortable with the messages put out by Ukraine's most prominent right-wing ultranationalist party. I had similar reactions from all the other interpreters I tried this material on that day. They hadn't heard anything about the Freedom Party before, but when they read its platform they found its messages unsettling. However, young Russian-speaking Ukrainians in the east of the country were not the target voters for this party.

A week later we got to meet the man behind the message in person. Forty-year-old presidential candidate Oleh Tyahnybok was born in the Lviv on the other side of the country from Kharkiv. He was descended from a western Ukrainian family that had actively supported Ukrainian independence after the First World War, and his grandfather spent seven years in Siberia for defying the KGB after the Second World War. Tyahnybok had great admiration for the Ukrainian partisan armies who fought against the Russians, the Germans, and the Poles in the 1940s. Like many western Ukrainians who remembered the punitive imposition of Russian communist rule after the war, he was no fan of continued Russian influence in Ukrainian culture, politics, or the economy. Tyahnybok studied medicine, but he was active in nationalist politics from his student days, and he had risen to be the leader of the Freedom Party in 2004. He was responsible for much of the image and policy it put before voters in 2010.

Our interactions with Freedom Party representatives were strained from the start. When I arrived for an interview with Tyahnybok ahead of my team, I apologized to the Ukrainian-speaking Freedom Party representative who met me in the lobby. I explained in my broken Russian that I was Canadian and only knew some Russian, and that my Ukrainian-speaking interpreter would be coming soon. However, the party representative just continued speaking to me in Ukrainian (although undoubtedly he spoke excellent Russian), as if to mock my poor language abilities.

Our private interview with Tyahnybok was brief. We took notes as we sat around him in a half circle in a backroom behind the auditorium. He leaned forward with his elbows on his knees and focused his intense gaze on us as he suggested that the national media was biased against his party and restricting his access to the national audience. Then we followed him into the theatre where a crowd of about 600 supporters had assembled. Three quarters of them were men, mostly middle aged or older, and many appeared to be low income, but undoubtedly, they were all ethnically and linguistically Ukrainian.

In a move I never experienced before or since, as we all crowded through the door into the hall, the organizers deliberately separated us from our interpreters and manoeuvred us observers into front row seats while leaving our interpreters standing against the auditorium wall. I couldn't decide whether this was some kind of punishment for our team's use of the Russian language or if it was a statement about the observer mission as a whole. But fortunately, having had that brochure translated for me multiple times the week before, I knew where the speech was going.

Tyahnybok was an extremely good speaker, engaging his audience with a compelling rapport and the confidential manner of a man among friends. Of course, the audience was a partisan crowd, and no one voiced disagreement with even his most controversial positions. They responded warmly to his simplistic arguments and his assertion that the problems of Ukraine were not political or economic, but problems of the soul. And they seemed to sympathize with his appeals to "we" the middle class, small businesspeople, engineers, and farmers that set them in clear opposition to the rich oligarchs and national politicians.

One of his platform planks was to put the ethnicity field back in passports and set up national quotas for ethnic groups in Parliament. He was adamantly opposed to dual citizenship and suggested that people who held second passports should be denounced and stripped of their Ukrainian citizenship. This sounded like a veiled threat against Ukrainians who also held Russian passports – estimated to be between a few hundred thousand and a few million – which Russia might use to justify intervention. It was a black and white "you are either with us or against us" stance that ignored the reality that ethnicity was complex for many people in Ukraine. There had been a lot of mobility within the Soviet Union, plenty of intermarriage, and high levels of bilingualism, leaving many people with a mixed ethnic heritage, and making primary language a poor indicator of deeper ethnic identity.

Tyahnybok's talk went beyond Ukrainian nationalist themes to stray into implied and sometimes outright racism. He complained about the power of criminal oligarchs in Parliament and the media, which his supporters would have easily read as a coded criticism of Jewish businessmen. Taking his racism local, he harped on about the role of the Vietnamese community in Kharkiv's massive bazaar and he alleged that illegal immigrants and foreign students – Kharkiv universities hosted some 10,000 fee-paying foreign students, many from South Asia and Africa – were dangerous, blaming them for everything from disease to drug trafficking, prostitution, terrorism, threats to women, and even "chocolate children"!

I was surprised at how much of this distasteful speech I could follow, but two hours of straining to understand without our interpreter was more than enough and we quietly exited. We had given the Freedom Party enough time to make their point, whatever it was.

II

By the time I observed parliamentary elections in the Ivano-Frankivsk region four years later in 2014, Tyahnybok's face was well known across the country. His party had exceeded the parliamentary threshold with 10 per cent of the vote in the 2012 elections and its members had been active, if not entirely constructive, in Parliament. In 2013–14, as a co-leader of the opposition faction, Tyahnybok repeatedly stood on stage alongside politicians Arseny Yatsenyuk and Vitali Klitschko to address the crowds at Kyiv's Euromaidan demonstrations. Freedom Party members were visible and active in the demonstrations, but they were just one of many groups that came out to the square. At the peak of their prominence, the small Freedom Party was assigned four ministerial posts in the government that emerged out of the revolution. However, Tyahnybok got only 1.16 per cent of the vote as a presidential candidate in May 2014. His ministers resigned after only four months in late July, and they were campaigning in the fall in hopes of increasing their seats in a new Parliament.

Ivano-Frankivsk was the heartland of the Freedom Party where they were second only to the Fatherland Party in popularity and had won nearly 40 per cent of the vote in some districts in the 2012 parliamentary elections. They also held a slim majority of the seats on the Ivano-Frankivsk city council. However, the Freedom Party's distinction as the anti-Russian party had disappeared after the occupation of Crimea six months before, after which most Ukrainian parties embraced an anti-Russian stance. At the same time, the Freedom Party's place on the far right of Ukrainian politics had been eclipsed by a new, more right-wing party, Dmitro Yarosh's Right Sector.

The Right Sector was born less than a year before in 2013 from a coalition of street fighters who came together under the leadership of Yarosh during the Euromaidan protests.[8] The members gained a reputation for meeting the violence of the police head on and supporting a radical ultra-nationalist agenda. They took on the red and black colours associated with the Second World War–era Ukrainian Insurgent Army, which brought back to many people's minds controversial allegations of ethnic cleansing and anti-Semitism in the 1940s. Reaching adulthood in the turbulent decade after the collapse of the Soviet Union, Yarosh had been active in nationalist politics for years before the revolution, but it was in the *maidan* that he made a national name for himself. The Right Sector had gone on to form a volunteer battalion that was fighting in the ATO. Yarosh received considerable attention from the international press in 2014, but he got less than 1 per cent of the vote from Ukrainians in the May 2014 presidential election.

In contrast with the older cynical audience at the Freedom Party rally in Kharkiv in 2010, the Right Sector team we met in Kolomyia in 2014 was young and idealistic. The oldest of the six was only in their mid-thirties. We found them in their one-room low-budget office happy to talk with us and share their position. We sat below a large poster of their leader, Yarosh, dressed in his fatigues with a big slogan reading "God! Ukraine! Freedom!" and an eleven-point election platform spelled out in the small print. The reputation of the party notwithstanding, there was nothing overtly ultra-right or ultra-nationalist in this platform.[9]

The party members were open about being a new group with small resources. Even in this haven for nationalists, they had only found sixty-three people to sit as polling commission members between 161 polls. And they expected to cover perhaps a quarter of polls with party observers on election day. They didn't have unrealistic expectations about how many votes they would get either. But they really wanted to talk about the bigger picture.

"We don't agree with how they talk about our party in the media. They are calling us racists, but we are not. We believe that minorities have a right to a place in Ukraine," explained one young man. "Our Ukrainian cause is like the situation of the Muslims exiled from Crimea, so we share their pain."

"Our guys are fighting alongside Jews and Georgians and Muslims in the ATO," added another. "We are all together in this war with the Russians."

"Of course, we do think that Christian values need to be promoted."

"And we would really like to see more progress on reforming the justice system. The corrupt justice officials need to go!"

"So, can you tell me how your party is different from the Freedom Party?" I asked. In this region, the Freedom Party voters would probably be the most likely to swing their vote to this new party, if they could see some difference. However, when it came to discussing the nuances of their party platform, the young activists had a hard time explaining the distinction between the two parties, beyond the obvious difference in their leaders. Half an hour later at the Kolomyia Freedom Party office, the party representative there couldn't do any better job at explaining the difference.

A lot of voters probably felt the same way. In the 2014 parliamentary vote, the Freedom Party got its best results in the country in the Ivano-Frankivsk region, but that was less than 9 per cent of the vote, and nationally it got less than 5 per cent. The Right Sector got less than 2 per cent nationally. However famous the leaders and their ideology might have been in the media, these political forces were not popular with the vast majority of Ukrainian voters. Another right-wing party that got a bigger boost from the Euromaidan events fielded a lot of candidates in 2015 in Kirovohrad.

III

"Everyone who has accepted bribes should be executed in this square!"

"He said what?" I can't believe my ears. Oksana is interpreting at this rally in the Kirovohrad central square for the national leader of the Radical Party, Oleh Lyashko. Lyashko is ranting enthusiastically as he paces about the stage in front of the memorial to the Heavenly Hundred. He's not a big man, but he is projecting a lot of energy and the crowd is lapping it up.

"He says ... 'everyone who has accepted bribes should be executed in this square.'" She grins, quite confident about her interpretation.

"Well Matti, I'd say that counts as 'inflammatory language,' wouldn't you?"

"I would say so."

Our reporting format for campaign rallies includes a standard question asking whether any speaker used "inflammatory, nationalistic, or xenophobic language." I rarely have to report yes to that question, but Lyashko is living up to his reputation as a rabble-rouser at this rally. Granted, executing people in the central square sounds pretty far-fetched in 2015. But a hundred years before during the Bolshevik Revolution and the Civil War that followed, political executions took place in squares like this in many Ukrainian communities, and Lyashko seems keen to invoke this bloody history.

Lyashko's campaign message isn't really written for the Kirovohrad Square. His speech is aimed at building up his Radical Party for national power, rather than local politics. He speaks out against the privatization of public lands and companies and in favour of higher pensions and lower taxes, and he has a lot to say about the sitting president, Poroshenko, and none of it complimentary. He doesn't raise a single issue specific to local government in Kirovohrad, and only introduces his local candidates at the very end of his speech almost as an afterthought. The Radical Party's candidate for Kirovohrad mayor, Rafael Sanasaryan, makes an extremely brief speech in Russian that does little more than reveal that he is a very weak public speaker. It may not matter, as most of this crowd are party faithful, not undecided voters trying to make up their minds, nor bureaucrats with their hands in other people's pockets for that matter. A couple of hundred people have come out, young and old and men and women, although we note that there are no women or youth on the stage.

But then, as I had seen many other times, while rallies are integral to an election campaign, they are rarely about winning votes. A political rally is a kind of staged ritual. The local party leadership are the warm-up speakers, who take the opportunity to show off their loyalty by introducing the leader as someone not far removed from the next messiah. And then the leader comes before the adoring crowd to make a long speech that demonstrates why he or she has made it to the top of the party (and should stay there.) And finally, after waiting tediously in the wings through this seemingly endless run up, the local candidates briefly get to stand on the stage, often silently, in the reflected glory of their leader before he or she hops in the campaign limo or jeep and heads off to the next event with nary a glance backwards. So, while rallies are designed to boost the spirits of the campaign workers, and they may raise the general profile of leaders who speak at them, based on my observations they rarely seem to do much to directly win new votes.

We observe rallies as much to see who is listening as to hear what is said. Rallies can provide a good indication of who constitutes the base of support for that party, and what kind of messages they are being fed, overtly and through any subtle subtext. Lyashko polled just over 11 per cent of the vote in Kirovohrad when he ran for president in 2014, so he has a reasonable local following, and his party has a lot of candidates running locally. He built his profile on the stage at the Kiev Euromaidan demonstrations and went on fight with the volunteer brigades fighting in the east from the beginning of the conflict, so he projects an aura of direct action.[10] Lyashko cultivates the image of an outsider, the antithesis of the parliamentary insiders and their corruption, and so he is attractive to supporters who want to drive change from the outside.

We met one of Lyashko's local supporters our first day on the job. We can't pick out the secretary of the City Election Commission, Sergei Osadchiy, in the rally crowd but he is probably here, hopefully deriving some encouragement for what could be a long road ahead for him in this particular election. This is more than you can say for supporters who turn up at the next day's rally.

The crowd at the Freedom Party rally the following day is mostly elderly, which isn't surprising given that it is the middle of the workday. The small group is dwarfed by their eight large flags that are flying the colours of both the Freedom Party and the Right Sector. But even with two parties coming together today, fewer than fifty people have turned up, so for all the hype about a rise of the ultra-nationalists after the 2014 revolution, this 2015 gathering feels more like a fringe movement at the political margins than one able to drive the mainstream.

The Freedom Party member of Parliament doesn't even need a small riser to be seen by the whole group as he drones on about the need for change at the national level. He goes on for so long that we have to leave before the local candidate can take the microphone, but we have already met him. Forty-five-year-old Sergei Kapitanov is a political neophyte, recently retired from the police. In the inevitable embroidered Ukrainian shirt favoured by nationalists, he seems an unlikely politician. But he is a realist, representing his party in the mayoral race, but also at the head of the party list for city council, where he has a better chance of getting a seat.

We can't meet all the minor mayoral candidates. There are three more on the ballot who have no visible campaign and who bear many of the hallmarks of technical candidates, but we can't track them down. However, we know from the media polls that there are two more candidates who we really should talk with because they have a serious chance at winning the mayor's job.

4.5 The Main Players

I

It isn't until week four in Kirovohrad that we succeed in getting interviews with the last two leading candidates for mayor, the two that could be best described as a "blue" and a "red" candidate.

We meet Artyom Strizhakov in a café on the Monday afternoon. He seems mature for his age and perhaps a bit intense. He favours a suit and tie for his campaign photos probably hoping to look older and more experienced than his thirty-one years, but he is dressed casually to meet us. We have seen him with his family on YouTube, so we know that his wife is deaf, which gives him insight into disability issues, and that his little twin daughters are every politician's dream of endearingly cute kids.

Strizhakov is already a sitting city councillor and is running for mayor as an independent candidate. He has a degree in finance and credit and while he owns a chain of mobile phone stores, he has long-term political aspirations. He ran in the 2014 parliamentary election as a self-nominated candidate where he came a distant third with 7,400 votes or less than 9 per cent.[11] But before the 2014 revolution, he was a member of the Party of Regions and Oksana tells us local rumours are circulating that he is now really backed by the Party of Regions successor party, the Opposition Bloc.[12] The blue colour on his advertising is darker that the Opposition Bloc blue, but he has chosen blue over all the other options.

Strizhakov is running a clever and well-funded campaign. He starts with a stealth program of anonymous billboards advertising a "new perspective" for the city. Then, at a flashy public event in a residential suburb, he launches his five-point plan for municipal development. He's backed by a big screen playing colourful graphics and he hits on current municipal issues like infrastructure repairs, stray dogs, garbage collection, energy conservation, and public transport. He brings on stage prominent local personalities to endorse him, including a doctor, a professor, a TV presenter, and a youth leader, and he takes questions from the audience of potential voters. It's not a typical political rally and we can study it all – through carefully edited clips – on his YouTube channel. It is a slick approach and far more innovative than the other independent candidates.

During our interview he invites us to one of his courtyard meetings later that week. Similar to door-to-door campaigning in Canada, Ukrainian candidates often meet with residents in the open space between their Soviet apartment blocks. On a Sunday afternoon about eleven people gather in their playground to hear him out and listen respectfully as he gives his speech and takes their questions in a relaxed, if not exactly exciting, exchange.

II

There are nearly thirty years between Strizhakov and his biggest opponent Andriy Raikovich, who is a fifty-nine-year-old businessman. It is a short walk for us the next day from our office in Matti's hotel across the street to Raikovich's campaign headquarters on the second floor of a 1970s apartment building. Raikovich's professionally-staffed headquarters on the main street is an indication that he has been nominated and is supported by the BPPS. Raikovich has also been endorsed by the Fatherland Party and Civic Position, so he has a firm hold on the red mantle in this mayoral race.

I already have some idea about Raikovich's campaign from my Facebook feed where short clips pop up with the candidate putting out his position or local citizens endorse him. While Raikovich is a two-term regional councillor representing the People's Party and is leading the current BPPS party list for the regional council, he was previously not well-known as a politician. However, he is a well-respected manager best known as the general director of Yatran, a major local meat processing plant. His campaign videos touch on many of the same issues as Strizhakov, such as improving public transport, communal infrastructure, and local schools. But he puts more emphasis on his business experience and his goal to improve the climate for local production and marketing.

When we meet him in person, he is relaxed and informal with us and, unlike the minor candidates we have met, he doesn't seem to overrate our importance as observers – at least at this point. He comes across as a mature establishment figure and we hear that he has been publicly endorsed by a number of prominent members of the business and arts communities. We have a pleasant casual interview and leave with the impression that this is a man who will appeal to older voters and people looking for a stable business environment.

When we check on campaign finance reports later in the week, we notice that none of the candidates report expenses for online advertising, although the main candidates are definitely leveraging up-to-date on-line strategies. Strizhakov and Raikovich are the only candidates making heavy use of online advertising and I see their in-stream videos popping up on YouTube. Following both of their YouTube channels, I can see that Strizhakov has generated an impressive 20,000 views for his main three-minute campaign ad and between 4,000 and 10,000 views for several subsidiary ads that are less than one minute. Raikovich's ads are all designed to be shorter. The most frequently viewed, getting 10,000 views, are only eighteen seconds long, and none of the others which have been viewed in the thousands lasts more than a minute. Of course, we have no idea how many viewers watch to the end of any of these ads, but we suspect that a video that is designed to get across the message in a shorter time may be more effective.

The local media feel this mayor's race is too close to call. A local poll identifies three front-runners. The pollsters think Tabalov and Strizhakov are neck and neck at 18 per cent and 16 per cent of the decided vote and Raikovich is not far behind at 12 per cent. All the other candidates poll at less than 5 per cent. But more than a quarter of respondents have not made up their minds. It's hard to know how scientific the poll is, but it certainly doesn't look like any of these candidates is likely to get more than half the votes in one round of voting.

Meanwhile, we have been hearing rumours from the start of the campaign that the blue Opposition Bloc and the red BPPS have some kind of backroom agreement, and that they are working more or less together to promote their common interest in a comfortable environment for big businesses to prosper. Specifically, the rumours suggest that the regional council will be a blue domain for the current member of Parliament Sergei Larin and his Opposition Bloc Party, while city council will be the red domain for BPPS under another local member of Parliament, Constantine Yarinych, and a mayor, Raikovich. Both MPS have suggested they will give up their national seats in favour of local politics, but we have no idea if we should believe that. By the end of week four, we have seen only superficial party campaigns and not a lot of direct competition between the red and blue political forces, so we think there could be some truth to this story. But come election day, will the voters support this clandestine division of power?

A Traveler's Interlude
Inside the Public Library

AS WE ARE OBSERVING A LOCAL ELECTION, I think it would be useful to get some idea about the standard of municipal amenities delivered by local government. Making my way home after a day of interviews, I pass a public library branch on the ground floor of my apartment building. I wonder, what kind of books do they have in there? My watch says a quarter to five, so I think I have enough time to take a quick look before they close. I open the door quietly – it is a library after all – and slip inside and start scoping out the shelves. I see a librarian out of the corner of my eye, but I don't disturb her.

I feel like I have stepped back in time. The walls are covered with decorative plaster tiles that look like they might have been quite trendy in the 1970s. They are painted a sad shade of beige in the room to the left of the door and brighter pale blue in the room to the right. It doesn't look like a lot of the books have been on and off these shelves since the Soviet Union collapsed at the end of the 1980s. The librarian is making a valiant effort with what she has; tidy displays and vigorous houseplants brighten the room, but the furniture hasn't been renewed in twenty-five years either. In a nod to Ukrainian culture, she has the requisite display of the works of the nineteenth-century Ukrainian poet Taras Shevchenko and another about the history of Kirovohrad. And in a poignant display titled "I Love My Library," she has tried to make the most of her vintage collection by asking, "What did our grandmothers and grandfathers read?" A question she has answered with yellowed items pulled from the shelves.

As I quietly consider the realities of underfunded public libraries, the library door bangs behind me. I look at my watch again and it is still only ten minutes to five, so I think the librarian must have left to pick something up before she closes shop. I continue looking around.

I am captivated by a surreal display at the end of the room about Yuri Gagarin of all people. Gagarin was the first man to orbit the earth in space in April 1961. His flight was a catalytic event in the Soviet-American space race and his name is still valorized all over the former Soviet Union. Gagarin was a great Soviet hero, but he wasn't Ukrainian, and you might have thought he had been replaced by more recent – and more Ukrainian – heroes. It says a lot about the challenges of developing a modern Ukrainian identity that Gagarin is still on the wall sixty-five years after his famous flight, alongside Shevchenko, who was born two-hundred years ago.

Recognizing compelling new heroes is a problem I have seen in all the former Soviet republics I have visited. Many of the Soviet heroes were actually Russians like Gagarin, and when the Soviet Union fell apart, the independent republics had to grapple with what to do with the heroes who were shared icons in Soviet days and are still widely admired, but who could not embody the new nationalism. By 2015, more than 400 people had been awarded the title of Hero of Ukraine, but none of them are on the walls here. Most of them are not really popular heroes; they are scientists, engineers, and politicians.

The exception is the Heavenly Hundred, martyrs of the Euromaidan Revolution who were added en masse to the official list in 2014 and are pictured all over the country. But not in this library.

Heroes who can bridge the national divides in Ukraine are hard to find. In January 2010, out-going president Yushchenko – who came to power on a wave of support from ethnic Ukrainians – made Stepan Bandera a Hero of Ukraine. Bandera was a west Ukrainian nationalist who led a group of Ukrainian militants that were active before and during the Second World War. Bandera is a controversial figure, revered by some as a nationalist hero who opposed Soviet rule and accused by others of anti-Semitism, ethnic cleansing, and collaborating with the Nazis. Newly-elected president Yanukovich – who had won with the support of many Russian-speaking Ukrainians – annulled Bandera's hero status in March 2010.

With these tangential thoughts running around my head, I realize it is time to go home and I go back to the closed door and give it a push. It doesn't budge. I push a couple more times before I realize that it is actually locked from the outside. And it occurs to me that the librarian probably isn't coming back until tomorrow. And it dawns on me that I have become locked inside a Soviet time capsule, a captive capitalist interloper to justify Gagarin's heroic Soviet mission.

In my purse I have a plastic card we were issued in Kyiv with numbers to call in the event of an emergency, including a twenty-four-hour security operations room in the capital. But there is no way I am going to set myself up for ridicule, or waste the security staff's time, by telling them that I have got myself locked inside a public library. Phantom headlines flit before my eyes: "International election observer detained against her will ..." No, no one must know! Instead, I call Oksana. She ponders a moment.

"Just wait. I have an idea," she says and hangs up.

Fortunately for me there are some English brochures printed by the regional government that I can read, and then I practice my Russian reading election coverage in a local newspaper.

Five minutes later Oksana calls back. "My friend from college's mother is the chief librarian." Ukraine is one of those countries where the right connections can prove to be invaluable. She continues, "I called my friend, and she called her mother, and her mother called your local librarian. The librarian is on her way back to let you out. Just wait."

Twenty minutes later the librarian returns, out of breath and apologizing profusely, and looking like she has been severely chastised for not only leaving early but locking an international election observer inside her library on the way out. I feel sorry for her. I hope they don't dock her pay. Judging by the rest of the library she's probably not making much to begin with. I head up to my apartment, calling Oksana on the way to thank her for making me a free woman again.

5   Buy the Votes

| Prepare the field | Win the votes | Buy the votes | Steal the votes | Invalidate the votes |

I

If "win the votes" is the legitimate way to win an election, "buy the votes" is the first step on the slippery slope towards illegitimate means. Vote buying is a kind of election interference that can take many forms, from secret cash payments, through in-kind gifts, to public government handouts timed to influence the vote. We heard many allegations of vote buying in every Ukrainian election, starting in Kharkiv during the 2010 presidential elections.

Pavlo was laughing as he hung up his phone. "That was my friend Oleh. He's very disappointed with the election today."

"Why?" We hadn't heard any complaints from the polls.

"He waited around the door of his polling station for about an hour, hoping someone would offer to buy his vote. But no one did." Pavlo chuckled again. "So, he had to give his vote away for free. He thinks he wasted his vote. He was sure he would score some cash today!"

Oleh wasn't the only voter who had heard that votes were being bought and sold in Ukraine. And like many people on a low income, he would have liked the money. We had heard many allegations that there was vote buying going on. A Reuters journalist caught up with a voter who advertised his vote for sale online for 500 hryvnia, or around $50 Canadian.[1] But while vote buying may have been happening in the background, we didn't see any signs of an open market for votes at the poll door.

Despite a lot of talk about vote buying, observers rarely catch people in the act of selling their vote, at least not in Ukraine. The next year, in 2011, when I was a long-term observer for the Kyrgyzstan presidential elections, one of our teams of short-term observers did see the practice in action. As they stood in the parking lot outside a poll, our observers watched money changing hands between two local men. They followed the pair inside the poll and watched as the seller collected his ballot and then, with the buyer watching over his shoulder, the seller marked the ballot and dropped it in the box. Then they parted ways. There didn't seem to be any doubt about what was going on and our observers were as shocked as we were that this financial transaction was so blatant. Like the majority of countries in the world, buying votes for cash is illegal in Kyrgyzstan.[2] However, local Kyrgyz poll staff was not surprised and made no comment on the violation of the secrecy of the ballot taking place under their noses.

Like most attempts at vote buying, the payments make little sense if the secrecy of the ballot is maintained. And even in those countries where I heard allegations of vote buying or other forms of pressure on voters, few people suggested that they doubted the secrecy of the ballot. So even if the voter had accepted a payment or gift, they should be able to vote for whomever they liked. Which is one reason why observers are always watching for more than one person in the ballot booth. Or people marking their ballots outside the booth or dropping their ballot in the transparent box unfolded so others can see who they voted for. These could all be clues that a vote has been bought.

The first elections I observed took place before the advent of the camera phone, but once that technology arrived, there was a new clue to watch out for – people photographing their ballot to send a picture to the person they had taken payment from. That would be hard to hide behind the small cardboard voting screens we use in Canadian elections, but in the large, curtained booths favoured in Ukrainian polls a voter might take a photo unobserved. Was that really widespread? It is very hard to know.

However, while direct vote buying may be illegal, public payments to voters around election time is common around the world. In the run up to the 2022 Ontario provincial election, I received a cheque in the mail from the Ministry of Transport for $330 – a refund of the license plate sticker fees I had paid for the two previous years. The refund was widely recognized as an attempt to buy votes for the incumbent Progressive Conservatives, but it was not nearly as generous as the $5,000 "retention bonus" they offered Ontario nurses around the same time.[3] The nurses' payments were to be paid out half before the election and half afterwards, which linked them even more directly to the election's outcome.[4]

While some incumbent politicians in Ukraine engaged in similar inducements through the public purse, none of the candidates for the mayor of Kirovohrad in 2015 holds an influential government post, so arranging gifts from the government isn't an option. However, it is not unusual for Ukrainian politicians to run charities that give out gifts – colloquially referred to as buckwheat or gretchka in Ukrainian – to potential voters.

II

"I got the information about my grandmother's food package!" Oksana, our Kirovohrad assistant, is out of breath from running up the hotel stairs. She knows we really want some details to back up the food package allegations. The brochure she hands us has an attractive photo of fruit and Ukrainian sunflowers on one side, and a letter from candidate Tabalov's charity fund on the other side explaining their "With Warmth and Goodness" campaign.

I turn the card over in my hand. "What did this come with?"

Oksana pulls out her notebook. "She got one kilogram of sugar, a litre of cooking oil, a litre of vinegar, a kilogram of dried peas, a package of bay leaves, a packet of condensed milk, and a can of tomato paste. And a package of cookies." She must have grilled her grandmother for the precise details.

"That's not bad gift!" The law considers a gift "vote buying" if it exceeds 5 per cent of the minimum wage, which works out to sixty-nine hryvnia or about five Canadian dollars.[5] I suspect the value of just one of these packages would be more than that amount.

"And she received packages like this before?"

"Yes, she says they gave out a couple in the summer months too."

"How did she get chosen for these gifts?"

"The head of her building committee was asked by the fund to identify pensioners in the building who could use a food package. He put her on the list."

I pass back the card so that Oksana can translate the letter from the charity. The core message is a thinly veiled attack on the ruling BPPS party's policies – and by implication the candidates associated with BPPS.

"Hryvnia devaluation, high food prices, and increases in utility tariffs are the results of the absurd policies of the current authorities that have pushed every third resident into poverty. That is why we have established a special resident support program, having an ordinary humane desire to help our fellow people." The text goes on to say that the fund, officially run by the wife of candidate Tabalov, will pause its charitable work while he runs for mayor. But they expect to be back to work after the election. There can't be much doubt that Tabalov hopes recipients of these packages will vote for him, rather than the BPPS candidate Raikovich.

"Do you think your grandmother is going to vote for Tabalov now?" I ask Oksana.

"I don't know," she laughs. "She's happy to get the free food. But I think she's going to make up her own mind."

6 Steal the Votes

Prepare the field ⟩ Win the votes ⟩ Buy the votes ⟩ Steal the votes ⟩ Invalidate the votes

I

For the most part, vote buying implies both a willing buyer and a willing seller. But if a party or candidate thinks their campaign is not getting traction and their attempts at vote buying are not finding willing sellers, they may abandon trying to persuade voters to their cause and resort to stealing the votes. Interference through vote stealing is incredibly rare in modern Canadian elections, and many Canadians wouldn't even know how it could be done. But in the countries where I have observed, most people I interviewed could tell me some of the many different ways that votes can be stolen, whether or not those techniques were actually taking place in their current election. There are many ways to steal votes, but if it does happen most of the theft takes place on election day or in the days immediately after. This is one of the reasons why short-term observers are brought in to watch the voting process at a selection of polls on election day and then observe how the votes get totalled up at the district level.

If they are in the right place at the right time, short-term observers may see votes being stolen by preventing individuals or groups of voters from getting on the voters list, getting to the poll, or being issued a ballot (what is being called out as voter suppression in the United States). This could include: voters left off the voters list; voters finding that their name has already been struck off the list before they arrived; voters intimidated or prevented from entering the poll site; polls located in difficult to reach places, and/or inaccessible to certain groups such as people with disabilities.

Observers might also see vote stealing techniques that add illegal ballots to the box such as: voters issued more than one ballot; voters issued ballots without proper identification, sometimes whole groups of them; the same voter cycling through the voting process more than once; members of the poll election commission filling out extra ballots and putting them in the box. Most of these techniques to steal votes are difficult to implement without collusion between voters and some or all of the poll commission members.

At the end of election day, short-term observers are on the lookout for corrupt counting practices that assign ballots cast for one candidate to a different candidate or remove them from the count all together. This could look like: poll commission members moving ballots cast for one candidate into the pile for another candidate at the counting table; people adding or removing ballots from the counting table; disproportionately invalidating ballots for one or more candidates; unauthorized people in the poll during counting, interfering with the counting process; whole ballot boxes being stolen or replaced on the way to a central counting place; false numbers written on the results protocol; or, results being falsified during tabulation at the district level.

II

The need to keep a careful eye on potential vote stealing means that in addition to observing the work of the local election administration and the political campaign, Matti and I are responsible for the logistics for teams of short-term observers assigned to our region. We start to prepare early. By week two we have already heard from the core team that we can expect about eight teams to cover our region. Each team will be made up of two international observers and a local interpreter and driver (with car). We are happy with this number. On several previous elections, my partner and I have been responsible for sixteen or seventeen teams, and it can be a lot of work to find that many interpreters and drivers in a short period and get hotels and local transport arranged.

The bulk of the short-term observers recruited and paid for by OSCE member countries are well prepared.[1] There is a quota limiting the number of observers from any one country in order to preserve the international balance of the mission. The mission usually also has funds to directly recruit a few observers from countries that cannot – or do not want to – pay for observers, to add to the mix. Sometimes short-term observer teams made up of staff from embassies in the capital join an OSCE election observation mission. These teams often come with their own interpreters and vehicles and already know the country well, so they can be easily integrated.

Parliamentarian observers are more controversial. Members of Parliament often join observation missions as short-term observers through parliamentary delegations, and long-term observers usually provide assistance with their logistics too. However, parliamentarians can be high maintenance, expecting more support and attention than regular teams, and sometimes they are not actually ready for the long hours of work that regular short-term observers put in. In my experience, parliamentarians rarely stay to observe the tabulation at the district level, which in some countries is the primary place where vote stealing happens. So Matti and I breathe a sigh of relief when we hear that Kirovohrad won't be getting any parliamentary observers.

As it is, with any group of short-term observers there is always the chance that one or two will not be properly prepared for the assignment. Short-term observers who treat the assignment as a holiday hoping to integrate a lot of tourism, or stay up so late partying that they risk oversleeping on election morning, or want to skip off back to the capital ahead of schedule, or even interrupt observing to meet up with long lost relatives, reduce the quantity and quality of observations the mission collects. But they are usually a tiny – although annoying – minority.

The districts our short-term observers will cover have been chosen by the core team statistician so that the combined observations of all the short-term observers will provide something like a random sample of polls around the country. Seven out of eight of our teams will cover districts close to or in the city so we book them in Matti's hotel. Only one team is assigned to a town a more than a hundred kilometres to the east of the city of Kirovohrad, and we find hotel rooms there during a field visit.

When it comes to recruiting the local staff, we divide and conquer. Oksana and I start looking for interpreters while Anton and Matti are looking for drivers. Oksana spreads the word and we put up an advertisement for interpreters on a notice board in the English language department of a local university. The core team has also posted web advertisements nationally. At the end of week three, I spend a Saturday morning conducting phone interviews from my sunny apartment with the most likely candidates who have submitted resumes. Then halfway through week four, I meet with a short list for face-to-face interviews.

Interviewing interpreters is one of those tasks that sounds like work but is more like fun because in the guise of gauging language abilities, I can ask them almost anything. While talking with these candidate interpreters, I learn a lot about the options for higher education in Kirovohrad and the expectations and dreams of young Ukrainians who have chosen to study English as a second language. They may live in a small regional centre, but these young women and men have high hopes that good English will help them build strong careers and contribute to the future of their country. To test their real-world abilities, I drag Anton into the office and have them interpret a discussion between me and my Russian-speaking driver where I learn some fun facts about his life too.

Meanwhile, Anton has been working with Matti to interview drivers and check that their cars meet our requirements. A week before the observers are due to arrive, we have a good selection of assistants and drivers lined up, with a couple of back-up people on standby in case of emergency.

Monday afternoon of our last week before the election, we drive Matti over to the Znamyanka train station as he has gracefully agreed to make the trip to Kyiv to collect the sixteen short-term observers assigned to our region. Tuesday morning in Kyiv, Matti attends a long-term observer meeting with the other long-term observers and then meets up with our newly arrived short-term observers for their briefing Wednesday and

Thursday. Managing a large group of total strangers when you have little time to get to know them can be a challenge, so Matti does his best to get a feel for the members of our team as he brings them back to our region. They all arrive back in Kirovohrad by bus on Thursday evening.

Meanwhile, Oksana and I are finishing up local briefing packages. This briefing report is the culmination of our month-long research project and summarizes our assessment of the local political situation and the preparations for the election that we have been looking at over the five weeks we have been in the region. The report also contains a schedule of observation activities for the five days the observers will be with us. To help keep our observers on time and on task, we lay out our expectations in some detail.

We also provide each team with information specific to their districts. This information includes: a list of addresses for all the polls in their district, so they can find them on election day; some local campaign materials, to give them some flavour of what voters have been reading; a list of local restaurants, so they can find a good dinner; a map of the city to help them get to the restaurant; and a hotel business card to ensure they find their way back again. And we throw in some of those election calendar cards for fun. We pack all the bits and pieces into plastic folders, and we are ready for our regional briefing session.

Friday morning, we convene in the hotel conference room and Matti and I give a presentation to go with all these materials. The seven women and nine men assigned to our team are from Albania, Canada, Czech Republic, Germany, Lithuania, Montenegro, Poland, Romania, Slovakia, Sweden, the United Kingdom, and the United States. They come from all walks of life and bring a wide range of experience to their assignment. Some are professionals on vacation, and some are retired, but all are committed to providing neutral reports on what they see to us long-term observers and to the core team in the capital. We conclude the briefing by introducing each team to their interpreter and driver, and they all head out to familiarize themselves with the districts where they will observe. It's basically the same schedule we followed when I was a short-term observer for presidential elections in Zhlobin, Belarus in 2010.

III

"Do you think we should count up the totals this evening?" the chair of the District Election Commission in Zhlobin asked the other members of the commission. "Or should we leave it until tomorrow afternoon?" "Oh, tomorrow will be fine," they chorused. "It's already 11:00 p.m. We're all tired." And with that they started folding up their big paper spreadsheet of results.

I jumped up. "Can I photograph that?" I asked, pointing at the big paper. If we weren't going to get an official protocol, I thought, perhaps I could at least capture the raw data in a photo. This was my first time as a short-term observer, but I knew that a key part of our job was to collect results from the district so that the core team could compare them with what was reported at the national level.

"No," was the curt answer as they locked the paper in their safe.

I was flabbergasted. I turned to my fellow short-term observer, Roman. Roman was a smart and energetic young diplomat from Slovakia. "They aren't going to add up the totals? It's not even midnight. How can they not add up the totals?"

"That is strange!" he agreed. "I've never seen that before."

And neither had I. Everywhere else I had observed as a long-term observer, if the tabulation took all night, the District Election Commission stayed up all night. However, it looked like calculating the totals was not this commission's primary concern. But this was Belarus, and there really was not any doubt about the outcome for President Lukashenko who, like some of his central Asian counterparts, had hung on to power since soon after the collapse of the Soviet Union nearly twenty years before.

While I had loved being a long-term observer in central Asia, I had never applied to be a short-term observer in those countries. It takes two overnight flights to get from Ottawa to central Asia and short-term observers are expected to stay up through the election night to observe counting and tabulation. I knew I would be jet lagged and exhausted for the entire week-long mission in a country that far from home. However, it is only one night's travel from Ottawa to the post-Soviet republic of Belarus, which is sandwiched between Poland and Russia on the edge of Europe. So, I had grabbed this opportunity to see an election from the short-term observer perspective.

When I arrived in Minsk, the Belarussian capital, on a crisp and bright snowy Monday, I discovered that I had forgotten to pack mittens. I pushed my hands deep into my pockets as I headed out of my hotel in search of a shopping centre. Hunching my shoulders against a bitter wind, I walked across a bridge over the frozen Svilach River and along the exposed shore past the huge Palace of Sports and down to a major artery. Most of the buildings were unfriendly socialist modernist structures, built after Minsk was almost totally destroyed during the Second World War. Looming over the intersection was a dramatic metal sculpture exploding out of the second story of the building on the corner. In the unmistakable style of socialist realism, the giant work of art featured a crowd of larger-than-life men and women determinedly striding out of the wall towards the inevitable victory of communism, with a deadly serious expression on every face. None of them were going shopping, I thought! Or perhaps that was the attitude you needed for shopping in the Soviet Union, an empire eventually undone by the perpetual shortage of consumer goods. A couple of blocks around this corner I found a shopping centre. I immediately discovered a hole in my Russian vocabulary. I had to mime putting on mittens to get directed to a third-floor kiosk where I was able to buy a pair of elegant purple gloves. With that purchase in hand, and on my hands, I felt ready for any chilly reception I might meet on this short mission.

Short-term observer missions are fast-paced. I met my short-term observer partner Roman at a mass briefing for 450 short-term observers on Tuesday. We traveled south to Gomel region on Wednesday for a regional briefing before heading north to the city of Zhlobin.

Thursday, we had a day to try to get some sense of our region. The familiarization day is often the one day when you can legitimately combine visiting election administration officials with a bit of tourism. Zhlobin had a population of 76,000 and was a major industrial centre. We drove by a steel factory that was one of the largest enterprises in the country. Our interpreter, Oksana Prohorenko, normally worked as a language specialist in the marketing department at the state-owned Byelorussian Steel Works, helping the factory negotiate sales with European countries. She was a friendly and professional woman, but I wondered if she had been allowed time off from her state job because she had been endorsed as reliable to ensure that we went home with a good impression of her country.

We drove around the snow-covered countryside visiting polls in neighbouring villages. The road wound past rows of painted wooden cottages surrounded by short wooden fences. The windows were hung with lace curtains and the frames and shutters were picked out in contrasting colours. The gables end walls were decorated with artful patterns in the wooden cladding. With the dusting of new snow it was clean and picturesque, and deceptively idyllic. Before we headed back to the city, Oksana suggested we should see a local war memorial. Always looking for clues to local history, I said yes.

As we got out of the car to approach the site at Krasny Bereg, I could see that this was not a typical memorial for soldiers. At the entrance, a rake-thin girl cast in bronze raised her crossed arms over her head as if to ward off a blow. The falling snow deadened our footsteps as we made our way past rows of white concrete desks up to a black board where the text of a letter was reproduced that explained the story behind this place. Sixty-five years before, during the Second World War, there had been a concentration camp here where the Nazis had imprisoned Belarussian children to use them as blood donors. To keep wounded German soldiers alive thousands of children were bled to death. The design of the monument was incredibly poignant: a classroom of desks for children who could not go to school, a playground for children who never got to play, and a collection of stained-glass pictures of children's art for children who were never able to draw. It knocked the wind out of us. There is no point in trying to rank which of the countless atrocities of that war were the worst. And it is very difficult to comprehend how human beings can slide into such indefensible depravity. Suffice to say that there were no dry eyes as we headed quietly back to the car.

By the end of Second World War, half of the population of Belarus had either died or been removed, making this the country that paid the highest human price in Europe in that war.[2] Perhaps this history of devastation makes it easier to understand why many people in Belarus may have continued to tolerate a dictatorship in exchange for relative stability while other countries went through upheaval and uncertainty in the wake of the collapse of the Soviet Union.

These sombre thoughts came and went from my mind as we sat all Friday and Saturday observing early voting in one poll in the city centre. Sunday was election day, and we visited a number of polls before observing the count at one poll in the evening.

The counting process was straightforward, and the poll commission almost fell over themselves to be friendly and welcoming. The chairman of the poll wanted to chat about our previous experiences, and I told him I had observed the presidential vote in Ukraine earlier that year.

"What did you think about that election?" he challenged me.

"I thought it went well," I said. "We didn't observe any serious problems. Most people voted the way they wanted to."

"We didn't think that was a good election," he declared. "The results were not clear."

"Well, it was close," I agreed. When the 2010 Ukrainian election had gone to a second round of voting, the difference between the winner Yanukovich and the runner-up Tymoshenko was only 3.5 per cent. But as that represented more than 800,000 votes, I felt the winner was clear. However, President Lukashenko of Belarus had never had a margin of less than 75 per cent of the vote in his elections – or so his carefully selected Central Election Commission reported.[3] I could see that by comparison, Yanukovich's win looked tenuous and the political situation in Ukraine uncertain. Later events in Ukraine would confirm the chairman's concerns.

We followed the chairman and his team as they took their results to the District Election Commission. Everyone was very pleasant there too, however our suspicions were raised when we saw them using a pencil.

In theory, the goal of the District Election Commission on election night is to accurately collect the results from the local polls to generate the district totals. But rather than using their computer to record the poll results, this commission used a large sheet of paper ruled in rows and columns. As the poll officials came in to report their results, the district secretary manually filled in this large spreadsheet in pencil. The only explanation we could imagine for using a pencil was that they intended to erase the results later and change them. But they wouldn't do that in front of us, which explained why they stalled the whole process at 11:00 Sunday evening.

Our suspicions seemed to be confirmed the next day. At 8:30 Monday morning, on the drive back to Gomel, we heard the results of the election announced on the radio.

"How can they know the national results already?" I asked Roman. "They won't have the numbers for Zhlobin until this afternoon ..." But then it occurred to me that the District Election Commission in Zhlobin was probably waiting to hear the national results and then they would use their eraser to make sure their district results supported the national picture. We didn't have any hard evidence of this form of vote stealing, but we could certainly infer that it was going on, and we reported what we had seen to the core team along with all the other observers that afternoon back in the capital. It turned out that short-term observers across the country had seen District Election Commissions recording results on paper in 40 per cent of the districts observed. This was just one of many shortcomings that lead the OSCE to conclude that "Belarus ha[d] a considerable way to go in meeting its ... commitments for democratic elections."[4]

IV

I heard allegations predicting vote stealing at almost every election I observed. And I saw some circumstances that left me very suspicious. But for a long-term observer to get their hands on enough tangible evidence to draw a concrete conclusion that votes have been stolen is rare.[5] However, we did get evidence on one mission in Kazakhstan in 2007 during parliamentary elections in the northern region of Kostanai. It all started with an innocent offer from the district secretary.

"Would you like a copy of our district results?" The secretary of the District Election Commission was young, friendly, and seemed to genuinely want to be helpful.

"Well, of course we would," replied my German long-term observer partner Jurgen. He looked at me, and I looked at him, and we both raised our eyebrows at our assistant Elena. Voting had taken place on Saturday and in most jurisdictions by Monday afternoon you might expect to see all the results. But none had been published and we had heard it might be difficult to get copies of the district tabulation from the local election administration. We were surprised it was so easy at the first district we visited. The secretary must have been acting on her own initiative. Certainly, no one had told her not to share the results.

She told us the chairman of the commission had already left for the regional election office. We had met the chairman a couple of weeks before and he had gone out of his way to be nice to us, taking us out for lunch and even giving us a tour of the massive mine where he normally worked. Employing about 18,000 in a city of 120,000 people, the mine dominated the local economy and likewise local politics. We peered over the edge of a grey pit half a kilometre deep where the massive ore hauling trucks at the bottom looked like very small children's toys. It had taken fifty years to dig that deep, and they hadn't stopped working their way down. From the pit, the chairman took us inside the huge Soviet-era ball mill. Standing on a metal scaffolding a few metres above the mill floor, we looked down a 600-metre-long hall housing a line of giant rotating mills loudly pulverizing the iron ore that would be shipped by rail to iron and steel mills in Russia and China. The massive scale of the mine and the mill said a lot about the importance of the enterprise and we learned that the mine produced half the industrial output of the region and 40 per cent of the region's taxes. Much of the rest of the region's wealth derived from agriculture.

On our way to Rudnyi and beyond, we had driven across an endless steppe, with no trees in sight and golden wheat stretching to the horizon. This must be what Saskatchewan looks like, I thought. But, although it might have looked like a farmer's fantasy in the 2000s, it had been a nightmare for the people who first broke this land in the 1930s. When the Soviet government collectivized agriculture, between 300,000 and 400,000 Ukrainian peasants were deported. Many of those who survived were dumped 3,000 kilometres east of home on these Kazakh steppes to build collective farms from scratch with minimal resources. The population of this region was now predominantly ethnic Russians, but after Kazakhs, Ukrainians remained a sizable minority.

Koreans were deported to the Kazakh steppes from the other direction. In 1937, about 170,000 Soviet Koreans were forced from their homes in the Far East when Stalin deemed them "unreliable" and moved them 7,000 kilometres west to the central Asian republics.[6] Our assistant Elena's grandparents were among 4,000 Koreans who were dropped in Kostanai at that time.

Forced labour and collective farms were Soviet history by 2007 and big agribusiness had muscled into their place. Spinning along the two-lane highway, we overtook a convoy of twelve new John Deere combine harvesters. No doubt they belonged to one of the vast corporate farms that dominated the rural economy, some of which planted as much as 50,000 hectares of grain in each of several districts where they controlled land. During a restaurant break, a Canadian entrepreneur heard my accent and wanted to chat. He had set up a local factory for farm equipment and sold out his annual production of 200 Canadian-style grain swathers in the first six months of the year. When he wasn't behind the wheel for us, our driver Igor also worked in agriculture. In the late 1980s he flew spy planes for the Soviet Air Force, but in the 2000s he was flying crop-dusters for the big grain companies.

Further down the road we passed a flowing herd of horses galloping across the rolling landscape. The magnificent animals running free seemed a romantic contrast with the farm machines. But Igor pointed out that they were actually livestock and destined for the plate. Indeed, when some local election observers had treated us to a dinner the previous week, the famous Kazakh dish beshbarmak was served: a platter of noodles and fried onions topped off with grilled horse meat, washed down with wine and vodka. However, it didn't look like we were going to have to do any horse-trading to collect the election results.

In the absence of the Rudnyi district chairman, the secretary extracted two pages out of a file and went over to the photocopy machine. When she handed them back to me I thanked her and immediately put them in my briefcase, nervous that she might change her mind. Or that one of the two older women who were listening from the doorway, members of the ruling party who were not election officials, might make her change her mind. So, we didn't look closely at the papers until we were back in the car in the parking lot.

What she had given us was the full tabulation spreadsheet, showing the results for each party in each poll, adding up to the district totals, and showing the percentage for each party at the district level. The percentage was critical because under the new elections law seats in the Parliament of Kazakhstan would be allocated under a PR system and a party needed a minimum of 7 per cent of the votes cast to get any seats. Both sheets were signed by the chairman and looked correct. But something else caught my eye.

"Something odd here Jurgen," I said as I took a closer look. "These papers have been faxed from somewhere else." Along the short side of the second page was the tell-tale line of characters in a boxy computer font that read in Russian: "From: Department of Finance, Rudnyi, Fax no: +31431 4-65-18, Aug. 19, 2007 01:19."

"Why would the results be faxed to the election commission from the local government finance office? You would expect it to be the other way round." The election commission was ostensibly independent from government.

Jurgen examined the papers. "We'd better go back and ask."

"But what if they try to take them back?" I certainly did not want to lose the results sheets now that we had them.

"We have to ask. We can't be making assumptions. There could be a legitimate reason."

"Hard to imagine. But you are right. We ought to ask."

So, back into the office we went.

"Sorry to bother you," we began, "But these papers seem to have been faxed from a local government fax machine. Do you know why?"

The poor young secretary suddenly looked flustered. "I don't know anything about that." She looked nervously at the two women ruling party members who had reappeared at the door, but they had nothing to add. So, we thanked them and left.

Our next stop was the office of the local coalition of opposition parties to find out what they had seen on election night.

"We had our party observers in all forty-two polls in the district. They thought the counting at the polls went pretty well," the opposition representative told us. This aligned with what we had heard from the two teams of short-term observers we had deployed to the town.

"We collected a lot of poll-level protocols," the opposition representative explained. "But in about half the polls, the chair refused to stamp the protocol, and a couple were even filled in pencil." Without an official stamp and inked numbers, the protocol wouldn't stand up in court if the results were challenged. A red flag went up when we heard that opposition observers were purposely given inadequate protocols.

"I was in the district election office for twenty-four hours from Saturday into Sunday. The District Election Commission worked all Saturday night," he went on. "But they shut the office for a break before all the poll representatives had brought in their results, including some of the polls where we thought our parties would get the most votes. That was at 7:00 a.m. on Sunday morning. And then I think the chairman went to a meeting over at the local government office."

This was news to us as our short-term observers had left at 5:30 a.m. to meet us at the airport back in Kostanai, the regional centre, at 7:00 a.m. Had local officials anticipated their exit? It would not have been difficult to figure out that short-term observers would have to be on the first flight back to the capital at 9:25 a.m. to attend the national short-term observers debriefing. I wondered if the elections officials had waited until the international observers were out of town before shutting their office.

"And the district still hasn't released their combined results," the opposition representative concluded.

Strange, I thought, because I have a copy of the district results in my briefcase. But we had to keep that piece of information to ourselves. Observers would not normally share information from one interview with another interviewee.

"Would you be able to give us copies of your protocols?" I asked. If we could check the numbers from the poll level count against the numbers recorded on the district tabulation sheets we had just collected, we would have concrete evidence whether there was – or was not – manipulation of the results at the district level.

"Yes. But we don't have a photocopier. We'll have to take them to a copy shop when we get them all together. I'll let you know when they are ready." Our interpreter, Elena, gave the man her phone number, and we left with fingers crossed that he would come through.

The next morning, Tuesday, our suspicions went up another notch when we were stonewalled at the three other districts where we asked for tabulation sheets. In each place, the district election officials told us they had no copies of their tabulation sheets or protocols of the combined results. They told us everything, all the paper files and even the computers, had been sent to the regional election office. No copies of the results were on display for the public to see either, contrary to the election law. Conveniently for them, they had nothing left to show us.

None of these district officials were pleased to see us. In one rural district, the chair of the election commission and a local government official followed us in their car until we had left their district. In another district, we could actually see the tabulation sheets in a file on the chairwoman's desk, but she flatly denied the sheets were available. She grudgingly gave us a signed protocol with the summary totals. That was as close as we got.

When an official refuses to show you district tabulation sheets, you cannot help but imagine that is because those district numbers are not going to match the numbers on the copies of the protocols issued at the poll level. But, unless you have the protocols from the polls, you don't have any proof, and the opposition representatives from Rudnyi still hadn't given us the copies they promised.

By this point I was fairly sure that the local officials had not intended us to get that copy of the Rudnyi district results and I started to get paranoid that someone might even try to retrieve the papers from us. When we arrived in the city a month earlier, we learned that a secret police officer had been assigned to follow our long-term observer work, and that he would be calling our interpreter Elena daily. Up until this week we didn't have anything to hide so we told her to be transparent with him. Now it felt like the situation had evolved. I took the two precious papers down to a small shop with a copier and had five copies made. Feeling a bit like a corny character in a B-movie spy thriller, I gave a couple of copies to Jurgen, and then distributed my copies between my purse and my suitcase and under my mattress.[7] This cloak-and-dagger move turned out to be unnecessary, but I slept better anyway.

On Wednesday, we continued our search for election results at the regional level. The chairwoman of the Regional Election Commission was a charming and worldly Russian woman we had met several times during the election. She had been seconded to the election commission from her regional government job, but always seemed under pressure to keep up both roles. On this day, initially she said she could give us something, and went away to collect her papers. After a long wait, she returned empty handed.

She sat down uncomfortably. "I'm so sorry. We have a technical error in our computer," she said quietly. After a pause she added, "You have to understand. I am in a complicated position." Finally, she told us, "You know, I was once an election observer myself. I was in the United States in 2000, in Florida." Of all the elections she might have observed, in all the states, Florida had the most complicated and contested US vote in recent years. The point she was making, I thought, was that she had seen first-hand the glass houses that western observers lived in. And so she was hoping we would refrain from throwing stones at her, at least.

When we went out for a farewell dinner that evening with our interpreter and driver, we still did not have the protocols from the Rudnyi polls, so I was beginning to think that our excitement at getting the district tabulation results was misplaced. However, at 9:00 that evening, as I was packing my bag, there was a knock on my apartment door. There was the opposition representative from Rudnyi with a stack of photocopies. I was too tired to do anything with them that evening, but I packed them safely with the district results sheets in my carry-on bag.

I woke up the next morning with a migraine coming on and the journey to the capital went by in a bit of a blur. When we reached the hotel I went looking for the core team political analyst to hand over our evidence for analysis, but he looked askance at my stack of protocol copies.

"I'm not going to have time to go through all of those for some time," he said.

I didn't want to wait for weeks to find out how the numbers lined up. Or worse yet, find out that he had never been able to find time for the analysis. "Do you want me to do it?" I offered.

"If you can, that would help."

So, floating on a haze of painkillers, I took the papers up to my hotel room and ordered a big pot of tea from room service. I got out the laptop and set about recreating the district tabulation sheet in Excel. Then I added in columns to compare the numbers from the protocols and started working my way through the pile of copies. I had protocols for twenty-five out of the forty polls, but by the time I had entered the first five I could see a pattern emerging.

Where the opposition parties had few votes on the protocols, the numbers in the district tabulation were not changed. Anywhere the opposition parties had a significant number of votes their numbers were reduced in the district tabulation. And at every single poll the votes for the ruling party had been increased. Across the twenty-five polls we had protocols for, the district tabulators had added more than six thousand votes for the ruling party, while deducting more than a thousand votes among the opposition parties. As we knew from the fax header, this manipulation had occurred on a computer in the local government financial department, not the election administration office.

Ironically, this manipulation wasn't going to change who had won the election. Clearly, the majority of voters had supported the ruling party, which matched our observations on the street. Instead, it looked like the person making the district tabulation spreadsheet had used formulas to ensure that none of the opposition parties had enough local votes to meet the minimum per cent necessary to enter Parliament. The best showing of all the opposition parties on the district tabulation was only 5.9 per cent, a full 1 per cent below the minimum threshold. It looked like the district officials felt – or had been instructed – that the ruling party should not only win but should face no opposition members in Parliament.

As observers we had been twice lucky: first we were given the district tabulation sheet, and second we were given a set of protocols from the same district. This was the only election I observed where I received such clear evidence of manipulation of the results. The report of our findings made its way into a footnote of the OSCE final report on this election and can be found on the internet to this day.

However, rather than feeling triumphant, I actually felt ambiguous. There is an undeniable thrill in catching officials in the act of corruption. But I couldn't help also feeling sympathetic. The election officials were local people roped into running the election. They were undoubtedly under pressure from the local political elite to create a good impression for the president, and that meant handing him results that reflected well on his ruling party. If that required tweaking the numbers to ensure that he didn't have to hear unwanted questions in Parliament, that may have seemed like a small price to pay to keep in his good books. However, at the same time it was known that the president particularly wanted a good report from the OSCE. So, they desperately wanted to prevent us from seeing their manipulations.

The election was a high-stakes game for local officials, and the tension was palpable when we met the regional chairwoman, but it must have been just as critical for the district chairman and all the other election officials we met. In a country where the ruling party exercised wide powers, their jobs and livelihoods could be on the line. On the other hand, election observation was a low-stakes game for us long-term observers. We would write our reports, leave, and never come back. They were going to live in that community for the rest of their lives.

V

It turns out that Kirovohrad region has a history of vote stealing remarkably similar to what we had seen in Kazakhstan. I wasn't there during the notorious 2004 presidential election, which had to be re-run because there was so much vote stealing across the country. But Ukrainian-American academic Oksana Shevel was there as an observer for the Committee of Voters of Ukraine. She wrote in some detail about what she saw in Kirovohrad's district 100, the site of particularly blatant irregularities.[8] In the first and second round of voting, significant numbers of votes were stolen from independent candidate Viktor Yushchenko and given to the Party of Regions candidate Yanukovich.

Even before the voting day for the second round of that election, it was clear that a fix was being prepared. The night before the election, district 100 fired more than 400 poll commission members who represented

Yushchenko. Then, on election day, multiple potential vote-stealing techniques were observed in the polls, including ballot box stuffing, excessive use of mobile voting, voters left off the voters list, individuals issued multiple ballots, questionable handling of blank ballots, unauthorized people in the polls, threatening poll staff, and excessive invalidation of ballots during counting.[9]

But the vote stealing at the polls paled in comparison to what took place at the District Election Commission. When Ukrainian observers in Kirovohrad compared the results written on the protocols collected by Yushchenko's observers from local polls with the results entered for the tabulation at district 100, the vote stealing was obvious. For example, where the count at poll 12 found 1,094 votes for Yushchenko and 630 for Yanukovich, the district recorded 642 for Yushchenko and 1,094 for Yanukovich. For poll 38, Yushchenko's 1,081 votes were reduced by the district to 268, while Yanukovich's 868 votes somehow morphed into 1,481 votes. And in poll 91, Yushchenko's 1,226 votes were knocked down to just 42, while Yanukovich's 758 votes multiplied by more than three to become 2,793.

In fact, only twenty-two out of 129 polls in Kirovohrad did not have their results altered at the district commission, and those were almost all polls where Yanukovich was leading. In total about 43,000 votes were erased from Yushchenko's results and nearly 36,000 were added to Yanukovich's. The scale of this vote stealing was breathtaking. The District Election Commission had reduced Yushchenko's actual votes by half while giving Yanukovich's nearly 40 per cent more votes than he had earned. In 2004, there were a number of political actors in Kirovohrad who had no shame.

However, under the watchful eyes of a large number of national and international observers like Shevel, the repeat vote held a few weeks later saw few irregularities and gave Yushchenko back the resounding victory in district 100 that he should have had in the second round of voting. He won 127 out of 129 polls.[10] Ten years later, the experience of both the bad second round vote and the much improved repeat vote in 2004 are not forgotten in Kirovohrad.

7   Election Day · Round One

I

As the Kirovohrad campaign period draws to a close, no one is harking
back to the election debacle of more than a decade ago, at least not in
meetings with us. Friday evening, while the short-term observers are
getting their first taste of the city, Matti, Oksana, and I are spread out
on the office sofa watching the final event of the mayoral campaign, a
live TV debate. It's hardly a Saturday night hockey game, but our bowl of
chips and soft drinks help build the atmosphere for a competition. The
TV host introduces this as his station's first attempt at running a local
election debate and he references the long history of election debates,
even showing a clip from the Kennedy-Nixon debates for the US presidency in 1960.

Only five of the fourteen candidates are included tonight. The three
leading candidates have been invited, but only Raikovich and Strizhakov have shown up. Tabalov has declined, claiming he will not get a fair
hearing, but then he places advertisements before and after the show so
he gets his message out without having to face questions. The other participants are Sanasaryan, the candidate for Oleh Lyashko's Radical Party,
Leybenko from the Opposition Bloc, and Atamanchuk, who I suspect
has been invited to give the illusion of some kind of gender balance.
They sit around the moderator in the big blue puffy chairs usually used
for the evening talk show. Beyond them is a studio audience of eight
journalists and local NGO representatives who, along with the candidates
themselves, get to pose questions.

Two of the candidates choose to answer in Ukrainian while the other
three speak Russian. As the interactions warm up there are some direct

and challenging questions. They want to know whether Raikovich can avoid conflicts of interest with his large business empire and whether he can make political decisions independent of pressure from his business friends. They ask Strizhakov – who seems to be surprisingly well-funded – about his campaign finance reports. And they want to know why he isn't running for the Opposition Bloc given that he used to be a member of the Party of Regions. They challenge Atamanchuk – who was previously associated with the Freedom Party and was rejected as a Self-Help Party candidate for this election – on why she keeps changing parties. And towards the end there is a surreal moment when one journalist asks each candidate whether they can work with the other candidates after the election. Raikovich not only says he can work with anyone but then offers both Leybenko and Atamanchuk jobs in his administration, on air.

As a finale to the election campaign, it is reasonably entertaining TV, and has provided an opportunity for undecided voters to assess five candidates, including two front-runners. But how many voters were actually tuned in to this low budget local TV station? Not many, we suspect.

II

Election day – E-Day in election observer parlance – arrives and the main job Matti and I have is to keep track of our short-term observers as they try to observe at least ten polls during the day. We are on our phones early in the morning, each calling four of our teams. Nobody oversleeps, but we check to be sure. Five of the teams start early, observing a poll opening before moving on to other polls. The other three teams start mid-morning so they will have more energy to stay up late at night covering the action at the district commissions.

The short-term observers spend about half an hour in each poll watching voters come and go and interviewing poll officials. They record their observations on paper forms with a special e-pen that digitally records their tick marks and written comments and then sends the information via a cell phone to a central server in Warsaw. This system allows the analyst in Kyiv to access the data arriving in real time and provide rapid reports to the rest of the core team summarizing what the observers are seeing across the country. The e-pens are a massive improvement on the fax machines, which were the standard way to relay poll observations to the capital for many years.

To capture some qualitative observations, Matti and I call all our teams three more times during the day, but they have nothing significant to report about the voting process. Predictably, counting at the polls takes a long time with so many races happening at once, and this has the knock-on effect of delaying tabulation at the district level through Tuesday and into Wednesday. We hold a debriefing session with all our observers late Tuesday afternoon and, while there are no official results yet, the general consensus is that our team did not observe anything like vote stealing in the region at this point in the election.

Later in the evening we reconvene for a farewell dinner. We have booked all the tables in the GorKom Retro Café. Located in a basement just off the central square, the menu declares it is a "Cultural Centre for Relaxation of the Intelligentsia" offering "special dishes for the future of the USSR." The café is decorated with a Soviet nostalgia theme supported by an extensive collection of communist-era ephemera. Under the glass-topped tables there are vintage coins, bank notes, postcards, postage stamps, and lapel pins. The glass cabinets that divide the booths house artifacts like old cameras, cigarette cases, and ceramics. The furniture and decor hearken back to the latter years of the Soviet Union, including a 1960s gramophone against the wall and a 1970s TV in the corner. Those ubiquitous busts of Lenin and photos of communist icons are on every wall. I'm not sure how much they are trying to cater to older people really nostalgic for the texture of their childhoods versus the younger customers who see irony in this satiric celebration of their parents' past. Either way, the food is tasty, affordable, and Ukrainian.

The next morning the short-term observers are back on the bus to Kyiv, and we breathe a sigh of relief. They have been a congenial lot, but it's always good to be able to send them home without incident.

8 Win the Votes Again · Round Two

| Prepare the field | Win the votes | Buy the votes | Steal the votes | Invalidate the votes |

With the first round of voting over and the short-term observers sent back to Kyiv, we spend the rest of the week cycling between various District Election Commissions to see how their tabulation of the poll results is coming along. It takes a few days to get official results, but by the end of the week we know that nine parties have enough votes to win seats in the new city council. None has a majority, so whoever becomes the new mayor will have to be a skilled coalition builder. About half of the elected city councillors have been on the city or district councils before, while the other half appear to be new to city council politics. A majority are between thirty-five and forty-seven years old, coming from the generation which made, or lost, their fortunes during the transition to the post-Soviet economy. Oksana and Anton recognize nearly a quarter who now hold senior positions in large local corporations and probably have a strong interest in protecting local big businesses. There has been a lot of change. At the same time, more than a quarter of elected councillors were previously members of the disgraced Party of Regions and these councillors are now distributed among six other parties.

Most importantly for us as observers, as we expected no mayoral candidate got a majority. Raikovich got the most votes at 27 per cent, but he's only a couple of thousand votes ahead of Strizhakov, who got 25 per cent of the votes. In that light, Tabalov's 20 per cent looks respectable. Tabalov is out of the running for the mayor, but he will get a seat on council as the local leader of his party. In a taste of things to come, Tabalov takes eight different complaints to court asking for recounts at individual polls. We observe a couple of Tabalov's cases, but his evidence is weak and he loses every case.

None of the other minor candidates got more than 5 per cent in the mayor's race, but several will also get seats on council through their parties' proportional representation lists. So, there will be a second round of voting for mayor in Kirovohrad. And with the top two candidates together only getting 52 per cent of the votes cast, representing less than a quarter of the voters on the list, it's anybody's guess who is going to win.[1]

The results are also out for the city name referendum and the favourite of the Russian-leaning population, Yelisavetgrad, has apparently topped the poll. The referendum wasn't a scientific poll and there are allegations of falsification. But, when we put the result alongside the strong showing for Strizhakov, a blue candidate and one who openly supported the Yelisavetgrad option, we get the sense that there are a good number of voters who lean towards stronger alignment with Russia.

The Finnish government is happy for Matti to stay on for the extra two weeks to monitor the continuing action. In contrast, I hear through the grapevine that the Canadian budget for this mission is tight, and that not all Canadians observing in cities where there is a second round may stay. I immediately send off an email to CANADEM pointing out that the cost of keeping me in my apartment is very low – less than $15 a day – compared with observers staying in hotels. I don't know if that is a deciding factor, but I'm told that I can stay until the second round is complete.

The round two campaign starts slowly. Poll commissions are re-formed with eight representatives from each candidate, but many of the poll staff are actually the same people who were nominated by other parties in round one. Most of the members of the city and district commissions are not changed. New ballots are printed and new voters lists are generated by the State Voter Register.

In contrast to the early start of the first round, we don't see any campaign activity from either candidate until at least ten days after the round one vote. Both Raikovich and Strizhakov thank their supporters via Facebook and Raikovich puts up a post saying that their two campaign managers have agreed that there will be no negative campaigning. They each have a few posters and billboards and one lonely tent at either end of the main square, but it is all very low key.

In-stream ads continue to pop up in my Facebook feed and on YouTube. We see that Strizhakov has a new campaign line which turns on its head Raikovich's earlier dichotomy of age versus experience. Strizhakov is now selling himself as a leader of a new generation and a man for the twenty-first century, condemning Raikovich for twentieth-century thinking. Meanwhile, Raikovich positions himself as heading a union of democratic forces, thereby suggesting there is something undemocratic about Strizhakov's bid and implying that all blue forces are undemocratic. However, neither candidate seems to be making much effort to increase turnout.

We continue to hear rumours that some kind of compromise is being negotiated between the red and blue teams in the regional and city councils. But that won't become clear until the regional and city councils meet in a few weeks and the level of cooperation becomes public. In the meantime, despite the superficial party campaigns, we don't see much direct competition between the main political forces. There is little analysis of the competition in the print press and most of the local press seems reluctant to take sides. We have to resort to online news sites to find an edgier or more partisan discussion. We are reduced to reading tea leaves when we note that one paper owned by an independent member of Parliament is only running ads for Strizhakov, while another newspaper owned by the blue Opposition Bloc member of Parliament Larin is only running advertisements for the red candidate Raikovich.

If there is a compromise, it is not clear where Strizhakov fits in the scenario. Surely he is not supposed to win the mayor's race. Cynics are saying that Strizhakov was only encouraged to run to draw away some of the younger voters from Tabalov and give the race to Raikovich. But Strizhakov has done better than expected. So, it would be premature to insist that Raikovich is certain of his win. There are also rumours that Strizhakov might be persuaded or enticed to drop out of the second round, and he does report that he has been pressured by unnamed sources. But as the round two campaign draws to a close he is definitely still in the race and on the ballot.

Before we know it, Matti is back on the train to Kyiv to pick up a smaller group of eight short-term observers who will monitor the second round of voting with us. While he is in the capital, local TV hosts a second debate in advance of the round two vote.

II

"I think Dmitro wants to be like Shuster," Oksana murmurs. Dmitro Kobetz, host of Kirovohrad's state TV current affairs talk show *We*, is a thin man with a long face and a tall forehead, and he looks down his narrow nose through rimless glasses at one participant and then the other as he moderates the round two candidate's debate. Watching Kobetz, I can see some superficial similarities between the local TV journalist and much more famous Savik Shuster.

Savik Shuster is one of Ukraine's most prominent journalists and political talk show hosts, and has a reputation for conducting hard-hitting interviews. His live TV shows help give Ukraine a much more dynamic media landscape than in many other post-Soviet republics. However, he isn't originally from Ukraine. Lithuanian by birth, he emigrated to Canada to study at McGill University and then lived in Italy before having several years of success on Russian TV in the early 2000s. Inevitably falling afoul of Putin's regime for asking too many controversial questions, Shuster landed in Ukraine after the 2004 Orange Revolution, and he has built a strong following on Ukrainian TV in the decade since. Big audiences tune in to see him bring politicians of all stripes before a live studio audience and challenge them with direct questions on air. Shuster's shows have moved around all the big Ukrainian TV channels as, one by one, he fell out of favour with the powerful oligarchs who controlled the national channels over his insistence on the editorial independence to ask everyone difficult questions.[2] Perhaps Kobetz thinks he is asking difficult questions too, but some of his questions seem more challenging for one of this debate's participants than the other.

Oksana and I are not actually in the studio for this debate, but we have made it into the green room. We watched the round one debate on the TV in our hotel office. So we were excited to get an invitation for a close-up view of the round two mayor's debate from the green room where VIP guests wait before going into the TV studio. The state TV green room has some of the requisite plush seating and complementary refreshments and, if the faded decor had ever had a real colour scheme, it might have been green. But like the rest of the state TV building, this room is irredeemably shabby, reflecting the vicious cycle of under-investment and declining viewership that presage an ongoing transformation at the TV network. When we visited the station earlier in the campaign, we heard that employees were demoralized because they anticipated that many of them would soon lose their jobs when this run-down state TV station would be converted to an even lower budget public service broadcaster.

When we arrived earlier that evening, Strizhakov had come over to sit beside Oksana and me on the green room sofa. The young politician looked nervous. It was hardly my job to reassure him, but it felt like that may have been what he was looking for. It looked like he was worried about the debate that was about to start, but it could have been something more. His team was on the other side of the room presumably talking about the campaign while strategically keeping the table laden with cheese and crackers and grapes between them and their opposition. Meanwhile, Raikovich and his team confidently kibitzed in the centre of the room. Everyone was very polite, but there was definitely an elephant in the green room. But what was it? We still didn't know when Strizhakov stood up and the TV producer ushered the two candidates down the hall to the studio where Kobetz awaited them.

Shuster made his name by speaking truth to power on all sides and perhaps Kobetz also aspires to be a local beacon of free speech and balanced journalism. The opening credits for the *We* talk show featured the words "freedom of speech," echoing the name of Savik Shuster's talk show. So, we are curious to see how the debate will play out. My round one media analysis showed that Raikovich was favoured by the station in its current affairs coverage. On the other hand, Strizhakov had posted a YouTube video of Andrii Bogdanovich, deputy head of the state channel, publicly endorsing him at the launch of the Strizhakov campaign platform.[3] Is the station leaning towards one candidate now? Or are the individual journalists, at risk of being cut loose, making their own guesses about which way the wind is blowing?

Kobetz opens the debate by reading the rules both parties had agreed to. The set for the debate is a dull yellow room and the three men stand in front of flimsy music stands that hold their notes. There are windows in the set walls, presumably designed to suggest they are letting in the light on the political process, but of course they aren't real windows. Strizhakov has opted for a tie with his suit while Raikovich and Kobetz both have open collars, but they could have all bought their dark suits at the same shop they are dressed so alike. However, one difference is obvious as soon as they start talking. Strizhakov choses to speak Russian while Kobetz and Raikovich speak in Ukrainian throughout. This should leave little doubt in the minds of viewers that Raikovich is aligned with the European-leaning parties while Strizhakov is playing to those voters who prefer closer relations with Russia.

Watching on the green room TV, it slowly becomes obvious to us that Kobetz had made his choice. While he mimics Shuster's direct approach as he poses questions to each man, Kobetz lets Raikovich answer first every time except for the final statements, where he gives Raikovich the more advantageous last word. Kobetz appears to have decided to let the debate be a platform for the candidate he thinks is going to be next mayor of the city.

Kobetz asks a lot of standard questions about leadership, the campaign, and municipal politics. How will you choose your deputies? What will be your first three steps in office? How will you use technology to connect with the citizens? How will you cooperate with business? Some questions, like improvements to transport and utilities, seem like a waste of time, as both candidates have very similar ideas. But then perhaps Kobetz is trying to subtly show viewers that choosing Strizhakov won't give them any better outcome.

Kobetz also poses some questions more likely to allow Raikovich to look good. He challenges both candidates on how many people they employ and how much tax they pay. Raikovich has an impressively large business while Strizhakov's business is small in comparison. Then Kobetz sets up Raikovich with a question about how he would form a working majority on city council, knowing that Raikovich has been advertising his meeting that week where he came to an understanding with enough parties to form a majority. As an independent candidate, Strizhakov is left to talk about situational majorities. Nevertheless, the main differences between the candidates – age and experience – would be obvious whatever questions were asked.

The overall tone of the debate is civilized and non-confrontational. But this subtext becomes more obvious near the end of the debate when Kobetz suggests that there have been negotiations about Strizhakov cooperating as the deputy for a Mayor Raikovich. Both men look embarrassed as they dance around the fact that they have recently met. They describe a very friendly meeting, but they claim there is no agreement. Kobetz points out that this is at odds with Strizhakov's campaign materials which allege that the young candidate is being pressured to drop out. Strizhakov's comeback is vague, and somehow he ends up defending the Raikovich campaign and blaming unnamed third parties. It is an odd exchange which leaves us wondering again how real the competition between the two candidates is, what exactly is going on in the backrooms, and what Kobetz really knows about it all.

Both candidates are stiff before the cameras and, even for an election observer, the hour-long debate is dull fare. We heard at our initial briefing in Kyiv that only a small percentage of viewers tune in to state TV, and we doubt that many of those viewers would stay tuned to the end of this debate as we had to. The show will eventually be posted on the state TV's YouTube channel, but I lament to the core team in my report that, like the first round TV debate, it isn't online before election day. While we have an intriguing glimpse of the backroom dealing that is going on behind the scenes during this second stage of the campaign, the impact of the debate on voters' choices is negligible.

9   Invalidate the Votes

Prepare the field	Win the votes	Buy the votes	Steal the votes	Invalidate the votes

Ukrainian politicians have a long tradition of complaining about what happens during their elections. Elections results up to the highest level have been determined by the courts' rulings on complaints rather than the total number of ballots in the box. Perhaps the most famous example was during the Orange Revolution in 2004, when a decision of the Supreme Court annulled the results of the presidential election and required a whole new round of national voting. But I know from my friends' tales in Odesa that complaints can lead to the winner being deposed in local elections too.

The 2015 Ukrainian Law on Local Elections allows many different parties to complain. Candidates, their proxies, parties, observers, election commissions, and their members all have the right to file official complaints. Voters can also complain, but only about violations of their personal rights. Depending on what they are complaining about, these parties can file their complaint with election commissions at the poll, the district, the city, or the national level and/or at the district or administrative courts. The bar to register a complaint is low. All that is needed is the word of one of these partisan parties – written in the specified form – that something outside the law has occurred.

The complaints system is fertile ground for parties that want to engage in interference as it offers multiple potential pressure points. For example, pressure can be put on the people who file the complaints, the people who present or defend complaints at election commissions or courts, the commission members or judges who adjudicate the initial complaints, and/or the commissions or judges who adjudicate further appeals. Even the people who report in the media on how complaints are handled may be influenced to present the story in a particular light.

There are many potential election offenses, including violating the right to vote, vote buying, falsification of election material and results, multiple voting, intentionally damaging electoral material, violating the secrecy of voting, campaign finance violations, and intimidating or abusing voters. Punishments can result in fines or even prison time. The system is supposed to deter electoral fraud, but it also leaves honest commission members nervous about the fallout if a spurious complaint is brought before a compliant judge.

Over my four elections in Ukraine, I saw complaints that ranged all the way from completely legitimate instances of violations of the law through to entirely frivolous allegations based on minor technicalities. Complaints might be driven by a genuine concern that irregularities have affected the overall result. Or they might be an attempt to reposition a loss as an injustice. A core team member once suggested to us that at the crux of the complaints process was the reality that many Ukrainian politicians would rather be seen as victims than losers. Even when the voters showed a clear preference at the ballot box, many losers chose to file complaints rather than concede defeat to their opponent. Of course, Ukrainian politicians aren't the only politicians who find it very difficult to admit they have lost.

II

By noon on the 2012 election day in Dnipropetrovsk, my Dutch long-term observer partner Bart and I had already been peppered with complaints called in by the main opposition parties in our region, Yulia Tymoshenko's Fatherland Party and Vitali Klitschko's UDAR Party. We noted down all the information for what it was worth, but we knew that a long-term observer team rarely has time to follow up on the details of individual complaints. Of course, the complainants knew that too.

But it turned out that luck was on our side in this election. In earlier elections, there had been concerns that short-term observers left before they had observed the full count at the district level. This time our short-term observer teams had been scheduled to stay in our region for a day longer than usual. However, the counting in these parliamentary elections finished fairly quickly. Unexpectedly, we had four teams of potential investigators with time on their hands and their interpreters and drivers keen to earn another day's pay. Early in the morning I shuffled through the stack of complaints that had been called in to us and picked out some for each of the short-term observer teams to check out.

We sent team 2903 to the UDAR party offices to follow up on the party's complaints about irregularities at poll 121115. Team 2904 visited several schools to investigate allegations of pressure on school directors to produce high results at school-based polls. Team 2905 was assigned to investigate the story behind a YouTube video posted by the Fatherland Party that purported to show ballot box stuffing at poll 121071. And team 2906 set out to find the lawyer for a Fatherland candidate who had complained to the prosecutor on behalf of a city employee about pressure from her boss to vote for the Party of Regions. By the end of the day our short-term observers had all reported back that there did not seem to be any substance behind any of these complaints.

At the same time, we long-term observers were looking at the poll-level results, all posted promptly on the Central Election Commission website. We could see that complaints about pressure on voters to support the locally dominant Party of Regions were undermined by considerable numbers of voters in every poll voting for opposition parties. Similarly, a complaint that inadequate voting booths affected the secrecy of the vote in poll 121015 was belied by the fact that opposition parties got their second highest results in that district at this poll. The evidence suggested that voters were comfortable that they could cast their ballot in secret for whomever they preferred. And the reality was the majority in our region chose to vote for the Party of Regions.

What was behind all those complaints? Looking at the local reactions, it seemed that many were structured to capture media and observers' attention rather that get justice through the courts. In the next couple of days, we asked the major opposition parties about their strategies for following up on these complaints and each one told us that their local complaints had all been forwarded to their national offices for decisions about which ones to pursue. This left us thinking that the goal of the complaints was not to get local justice or redress for specific violations, but rather to use the complaints to support the parties' national strategic goals.

Eventually, one Fatherland representative directly told us that their overall strategy was to weaken the ruling Party of Regions by undermining the government's relations with the European Union by making the election look unfair. It was clear to us that they saw international observers as a key tool in this strategy. The flurry of election day complaints – none of which turned out to be serious and many of which were clearly spurious – were part of this strategy.

It was frustrating to realize that these opposition parties were manipulating the complaints system to undermine the credibility of the outcome of the election and undermine the legitimacy of the overall results before the international community. It was a cynical approach to take, and without the unexpected backup of our short-term observer teams to investigate more of the complaints, we might not have seen through the misinformation. As it was, we were able to give a more accurate report to our core team about what was really behind the complaints in our region.

Based on experiences like this, by 2015 I knew that the election complaints process was a strategic battlefield where Ukrainian parties frequently continued their fight, long after all the ballots were marked and counted.

10 Complain to the Bitter End

|

15 November 2015, local elections round two, E-Day

If you ask me which way I think the election is going on the morning of the second round of voting in Kirovohrad, I'm ready to put my money on Raikovich. I don't think he is going to get a landslide, but he is the older, more experienced candidate and he just looks more credible to me as the leader of a city. But as an older woman I admit to a bias for age. Raikovich definitely came out on top in the TV debate and his advertising plays to the voters who desire stability. Strizhakov's messaging, on the other hand, is more about change and a new vision. No doubt he will maintain the voters he won over in the first round, but can he really pick up enough of the votes that had gone to minor candidates in the earlier vote to take a lead this time? I don't know, but I do know there is a possibility that the results will be close.

I check early morning texts while still in bed, confirming that two of our short-term observer teams have arrived at their chosen polls to observe the opening procedures. Then I roll over to catch another hour's sleep, knowing that whatever the results, we will have another long night ahead of us. Later in the morning we hear from the other two short-term observer teams that they have started their observations. They have a later start as they are assigned to observe later into the early morning hours at the two District Election Commissions.

Before noon our long-term observer team meets for coffee, and then we follow first Oksana and then Anton to their polls so that they can vote and we can get in a couple of poll observations to add to the short-term observer's poll reports from Kirovohrad. In the mid-afternoon we drive over to Novenska on the outskirts of the city to do some observations at polls there, and we are back in the centre of the city in time to attend a press conference at the NGO-run press centre by 5:00 p.m. Complaints about the voting process are minimal and candidate Raikovich says he thinks any violations are "sporadic and could not affect the election results."[1]

We call in reports three times during the day to the core team, but really we have nothing to remark on. Voting goes smoothly and the counting at the polls and the tabulation at the District Election Commissions that our short-term observers observe seem straightforward. And we don't hear any complaints from either campaign team or other observers during the day.

However, by the time we send in our final report for election day at midnight, we have already heard rumours that the race is incredibly close. When we talk with our short-term observers at the District Election Commissions, they have heard from local journalists that the candidates' parallel counts suggest that the results are too close to call. And then, at ten minutes to midnight, a national online media site goes public with a report that Strizhakov is claiming victory with a lead of only 400 votes.

I crash into bed, my head spinning with the potential ramifications of a margin that small. It is hard to imagine that Raikovich's team will give up if they are that close to winning, and I fall asleep with images of complaints documents and court cases dancing through my brain.

II

As I drift off to sleep, on the other side of Kirovohrad at poll 867, representatives for Raikovich are chewing on their pens and scribbling on forms. Poll 867 is located in the premises of Professional Technical School No. 4 on Marshal Koneva Boulevard and serves a dense neighbourhood of uniform nine-story apartment buildings on the western edge of the city. The school is walking distance from a large area of the garden plots that border on the farm fields that stretch to the horizon on all sides of the city. A majority of the neighbourhood's residents voted for Strizhakov in the first round of voting, so this could be expected to be his stronghold again in the second round.

The chair of poll 867, M.T. Kirichenko, a short middle-aged woman, was nominated by Raikovich's party. The secretary, Olga Zeifert, a taller and younger woman, has been appointed by Strizhakov. But neither woman makes a big deal out of party allegiances, and they work collegially with all their commission members.

Election day has been quiet at poll 867. Only 653 voters turned out from a list of 2,262, which makes for only a 29 per cent turnout. With so few votes to count it doesn't take long for the commission to conclude that Strizhakov has won their poll with 484 votes to Raikovich's 150. Observers for each candidate are immediately on their mobile phones, reporting the results to each candidate's parallel counts.

Not long after they call in their results, Raikovich's representatives in poll 867 receive instructions back from their campaign team. They urgently need to find some mistakes to complain about. But what mistakes, they wonder? Oh, surely there must have been something, they are advised. No poll is perfect.

And so, they put their heads together and they write down the only violations they can think of. There was one old woman, probably short-sighted, who leaned on a windowsill in the open to take advantage of the sunlight as she marked her ballot. Technically, she could have violated the secrecy of the vote if she filled in her ballot outside the booth. Then there was that mother who picked up her child and held her over the ballot box so the kid could drop in the mother's ballot. It is not legal for anyone not on the voters list to deposit a ballot in the box. Technically that is a mistake too.

A few blocks south of poll 867, poll 861 is located on Kosmonavta Popova Street, and serves the same neighbourhood of grey 1970s apartment blocks. Chairwoman Zhabchik and her secretary Shaligina were on the job early. Perhaps they expect Strizhakov to lead again at their poll, but their concern is not who the voters would vote for but ensuring that they run the voting process according to the law.

Voting in poll 861 is unremarkable, but a couple of minor complaints are filed around 10:00 a.m. by the same two women representing Raikovich. In the evening pressure heats up though. At 6:30 p.m. Oksana Frosniak's husband, Vitali Frosniak, registers at the poll as a journalist with Raikovich's party newspaper, but rather than gathering information for a media report he files a complaint. Then, after the counting starts, his brother Ruslan Frosniak, deputy chair of Raikovich's party, arrives. Ruslan does not register but he proceeds to sign three complaints between 9:50 and 11:50 pm. So, by midnight there are six complaints filed at poll 861, four of them by Frosniaks. Perhaps an alarm has sounded elsewhere because at ten minutes after 11:00 p.m. the poll commission registers two observers for Strizhakov arriving at the poll.

At polls 852, 862, 863, and 864 similar minor technicalities draw complaints. Isn't there supposed to be an information table? Were the ballots counted in the exact order specified in the regulations? Does the chairwoman get the full commission's decision on every invalid ballot eliminated? There are so many ways that a commission can fall afoul of the law if you really look for them. Usually, such technicalities aren't worth complaining about. But Raikovich's supporters are asked to produce some complaints and that is what they do.

Back at poll 867, as the commission is finishing packaging all their poll materials, Raikovich's representatives take their papers up to Chairwoman Kirichenko and ask her to register them. Kirichenko looks at them askance, but she follows the procedures and registers the complaints. However, she does not ask the rest of the commission to rule on the complaints yet. First, they need to prepare eighteen copies of the results protocols and deliver them. And it turns out that writing protocols will take up the rest of the night.

In the early hours of the morning, Kirichenko and her secretary Zeifert pile into a car and head out in the dark. They take their white tamper-proof bag, filled with sealed packages of all their ballots and papers and tied closed with string, to the Kirovska District Election Commission office to deliver their results. They are all tired and the other poll commission members head home soon after the leaders leave. At the District Election Commission Kirichenko gets a shock – the first of many it turns out.

The District Election Commission takes some time examining 867's protocols. They don't find anything wrong with the numbers though. The math is all clear and correct. However, eventually someone notices that the poll has used protocol forms intended for a village poll commission not a city poll commission. It is a very minor issue that could have no impact on the results. Nevertheless, Kirichenko and Zeifert are instructed to go back and create new protocols on the correct forms. The other commission members have all gone home, they point out. Then ask them to reconvene, the district commission tells them. The new protocols have to be signed by everyone.

With sighs of exhaustion the women from poll 867 head back to the school, dialling commission members on their mobiles as they go. When they return later with a second set of corrected protocols, they are again closely examined and this time someone points out that some of the copies have a different time on them – by five minutes. So, back they trudge again and create a third set with the same time on all of them. And when they came back with this third set they find that someone at the district commission has given them templates designed for a district commission not a poll commission. So, they are sent back to create a fourth set of protocols! This fourth set is finally accepted, but not before mid-morning the next day. This is a huge pain for poll 867's commission members, but it works well for others.

Without the official protocols for poll 867's results there will be some delay before Kirovska District Election Commission can total up the results for their district. And without the Kirovska district results there will be an even longer delay before the City Election Commission can total the results for the city. And those delays conveniently create time for both campaign teams to consider their next steps.

III

16 November 2015, E-Day+1

I look at the online reports as soon as I wake up Monday morning, and I can see that my fears of the previous night are not unfounded. "Closest race in Ukraine hangs on the results of one poll," is the title Matti and I choose for our 7:00 a.m. report to the core team. And reactions are coming in fast.

Our short-term observer team that covered the Leninski District Election Commission tells us that Leninski had collected the results for all forty-five of their polls, handed the short-term observers a printout of the results, and closed up shop by 5:00 a.m. The commission actually sealed the doors of their office until 2:00 this afternoon. The small Nove district commission has quickly brought in their results too. I can almost hear a collective sigh of relief from these two district commissions that it will now be difficult to drag them into any attempts to manipulate the razor thin difference in the results. All the focus now settles on the Kirovska District Election Commission.

Meanwhile in Kyiv, the core team holds a morning press conference to release its preliminary statement on the conduct of the elections. The statement raises concerns that business interests have been influencing the election process across most of the twenty-nine mayoral races being observed, and many candidates have focused on building local party coalitions rather than reaching out to voters. As we have seen in Kirovohrad, there was little active campaigning in most cities and there are concerns about the independence of District Election Commission members. But the statement does commend the dedication of poll staff during voting and counting. However, as the statement has to be written early in the morning it has nothing to say about the races such as Kirovohrad where counting and tabulation are ongoing and court proceedings haven't even started yet. In the meantime, the statement recommends readers stay tuned for the final report, which won't be released for at least eight weeks. Eight weeks is a long time in politics.

We print off copies of the statement to share with people we meet during the day, although no one involved with the election has time to read through a ten-page document today. At our first stop for the morning at the City Election Commission, Secretary Osadchiy looks resigned as he lays out the math for us, in case we hadn't figured it out. All the polls that are under attack with complaints are polls where Strizhakov has a strong lead. We also bump into Strizhakov's proxy at the city commission who explains that poll 867 is the prime target because eliminating that poll will take away the maximum votes from Strizhakov while eliminating the minimum votes from Raikovich.

Neither man says it outright – they probably assume we have noticed – that while the chair and deputy of the city commission represent different parties that competed for seats during the first round of the election, both of their parties backed Raikovich for mayor. So as a political crisis is developing, Chaika and Frosniak are now on the same side, leaving Osadchiy a lonely neutral man among the three leaders of the commission.

Moving on to the Kirovska district commission offices we find another of our short-term observer teams still on the job. The atmosphere is tense, and everyone looks exhausted and under pressure. A commission member tells us that Raikovich's proxies have chosen to take their complaints about the errors in the voting process at poll 867 to the Kirovska District Court, so we head to the court in search of copies of the complaints.

After a quick lunch we attend another press conference at the NGO press centre where the apparent winner, Strizhakov, appears in person. Raikovich is not there, leaving the city chair for BPPS to defend his position. Strizhakov seems surprisingly non-confrontational and conciliatory, but he does not rule out using the courts to defend his results if necessary.

Meanwhile, around the same time that we are observing the calm candidate meet the press, our short-term observers at the Kirovska district commission offices are getting a different picture of his campaign team. Strizhakov representatives turn up at the commission offices with some of the poll 867 commission members and a heated argument breaks out about who should really be complaining about what actually happened in poll 867 the night before. Unsubstantiated allegations are thrown around about unauthorized people from both sides being in the poll during the night. Eventually, poll 867 members are sent away to write an official report about what occurred in their poll. In contrast with the candidate's demeanour at the press conference, the gloves have definitely come off at the District Election Commission.

Our short-term observers go on taking notes and photographing documents for us, but eventually they have to leave. We have scheduled an official debriefing for our four teams of short-term observers at 3:30 p.m., and we need to collect all their impressions and photo evidence before they head back to Kyiv. In a quieter election, we would have also joined them for a farewell dinner, but it is obvious that this time it is more important for us to return to the District Election Commission where a meeting is scheduled for 5:00 p.m.

Back at the Kirovska district commission office for a second time that day, we are surprised to learn that the Raikovich team has withdrawn the complaints they had taken to the court that morning. However, they are now presenting a new complaint to the District Election Commission alleging that the poll 867 polling commission had not counted their different types of ballots – the unused ballots, the used ballots, the spoiled ballots, etc. – in the correct order. In response, Chairwoman Kirichenko presents her report and documents laying out her version of what had happened in her poll the night before.

The chairman of the district commission has been changed since the first round of the election. Volodymyr Gluhy is a solid man with a consciously serious demeanor. He doesn't seem to be really enjoying his position and is often impatient when he sees us international observers coming to ask what he deems unnecessary questions. This evening he defers to Deputy Chair Bezzubov who reads out the complaint and poll 867's response for discussion, but he doesn't get far before Chairman Gluhy – with considerable drama – collapses.

We all hurry out into the entrance hall while emergency services are called in. As a paramedic in a high visibility vest moves in to work on Gluhy, Matti, Oksana, and I hang about in the corridor and speculate. Is this all an act to gain more breathing space? Or is it possible that the pressure on the Gluhy to find a way to change the results has triggered a genuine attack of high blood pressure or worse? It could have been either or both for that matter. I don't envy him his position.

We are still whispering together when Bezzubov comes out and announces that the district commission will be adjourning their work for twenty-four hours, by which time Gluhy thinks he will have recovered. We note to ourselves that even without Gluhy, the commission has enough members to maintain their quorum and continue working. But that is not part of the plan, it seems. Secretary Lokareva then announces that she has heard that there are another twenty-three complaints being prepared. These mystery complaints will have to be dealt with before they can complete their district results protocol, so clearly nothing can be resolved this evening. Strizhakov's proxies seem to know nothing about these additional complaints, which leaves only one party that could be behind them, if they really exist.

Meanwhile, Oksana has been poking away at her phone, reading the internet chatter about the growing scandal of the delayed election results. Her reading of the social media buzz suggests that the battle developing between the mayoral candidates is really a proxy war between two regional politicians who headed factions in the regional council that stand behind either candidate. If correct, that would mean that the strings that are being pulled start far above any of the election commission members.

As the meeting breaks up, we take the chairwoman of poll 867 aside to ask what she thinks about this whole situation. Kirichenko is a mature and thoughtful woman, and despite being tired and harassed she remains sincere and dignified.

"I took an oath when I was appointed as a chairperson and I committed to do everything according to the law. And I am standing by that oath," she tells us. "But I am ashamed and embarrassed with the party that appointed me." Kirichenko was appointed by Raikovich's party. "They are putting a lot of pressure on our poll commission by making all these complaints about ridiculous irregularities. Like the child dropping their parent's ballot in the box! For goodness sakes, everyone saw President Poroshenko's grandchildren drop his ballot in the box for him on national TV in the morning. How can that be something to file a complaint about?" Clearly, she does not agree that there were irregularities at her poll, and it doesn't look like she is going to cave to pressure to change her results, regardless of who has appointed her.

We return to the hotel to send off the short-term observers on the evening train to Kyiv. We have to report to the core team that we do not anticipate final results from Kirovohrad for another day at least. We all know that the legal deadline for publishing the election results is midnight five days after election day, so there seems to be plenty of time to sort out a conclusion. Nevertheless, E-Day+1 ends leaving Raikovich's team with no opportunity to challenge the results in Leninski or Nove districts, and the Kirovska district commission delaying dealing with the complaint against poll 867.

IV

17 November 2015, E-Day+2

They're not counting the unused ballots, I think. I lean across Oksana and hiss at Matti, "Aren't they going to count the unused ballots?"

Matti quietly raises his eyebrows. He can see where this is heading.

"Is it some kind of a setup?" I ask.

"What?" asks Oksana.

"It's ..." I pause. I look at my neighbour on the right. The young woman who is a proxy for Strizhakov plunked herself down beside me while we were staking out our seats earlier. She clearly thinks it will look good for her cause to be associated with the international observers.

"I'll explain after," I tell Oksana. I realize I have no idea whether the proxy understands English or not. I have been caught out before, making what had I meant to be a private comment in English, only to realize later that someone around me understands English quite well. Of course, I have occasionally benefited from the same ignorance, catching some comments in Russian that the speakers incorrectly assumed I wouldn't understand. Election observation isn't supposed to be a cloak-and-dagger game tricking people about what you can understand. But accidental eavesdropping can happen.

Regardless, I have to keep quiet. An election observer's job is to observe and record. You should never be seen to interfere in the process. Even if you see an election official not following proper procedure – deliberately or by mistake – it is not your job to interfere and correct them. That is the responsibility of the local stakeholders. So, I have to sit on my hands and keep my mouth shut. Stoic Matti, to his credit, is able to do this more calmly. But we are both getting tired by this point after more than three hours of observing the tedious process.

The recount of the ballots from poll 867 was scheduled to begin Tuesday at 5:30 p.m. at the Kirovska district office. We didn't want to miss anything so we were on time, but the actual counting didn't get started until 8:00 p.m. A jumbled pyramid of seventy-three white tamper-resistant bags of ballots from seventy-three polls towered behind the secretary's desk at one end of the room. The seventy-fourth bag from poll 867 was placed prominently apart on a chair by the wall, and a couple of green desks were pushed together in the centre of the room.

The meeting room gradually filled up. All members of the Kirovska District Election Commission filtered in, many of them coming directly from their day jobs. All the members of polling commission 867 were there also, with Chairwoman Kirichenko, Secretary Zeifert, and a third member standing near the front. Neither candidate was there but each had sent a proxy to represent them. The media was out in force, with cameras on tripods from both TV stations, and we recognized reporters from the key online press sites. Ukrainian civil society observers from OPORA and CVU arrived. Mikhail and Nino from ENEMO also took their seats. In total, we made up an audience of about thirty people, all absorbed with the piece of political theatre about to take place. It was high stakes game, and everyone understood that the outcome of the recount had the potential to change the overall election result.

Chairman Gluhy, who had seemed to be a death's door the previous afternoon, was back in the saddle and ostensibly presiding. He brusquely instructed everyone to put their phones on silent and then promptly ejected someone who answered a ringing phone. However, after that he handed the process over to Deputy Chair Bezzubov, and then spent the entire evening on the phone himself with an off-site caller who appeared to be very interested in the progress of the recount.

Bezzubov supervised other members of the District Election Commission as they brought the poll 867 bag over to the green tables, opened it, and pulled out a number of brown paper packages one by one, each wrapped in scotch tape with signed documents fixed to the outside. The three key members of poll 867's commission carefully perused each package and declared that nothing appeared to have been tampered with since they sealed the bag two nights before. A member of the District Election Commission then opened the package of ballots for each candidate. While we all watched in silence, he held up each of the 650 ballots cast, one by one, for the room to see.

The District Election Commission members seemed keen to demonstrate that they were taking the whole process seriously. From time to time a commission member would raise a question about the validity of an individual ballot. Perhaps the "X" the voter marked had strayed slightly outside the little box on the ballot. Or maybe there was some other unexplained mark on the ballot. The commission members would then make show of carefully examining the ballot. Eventually they eliminated a total of twelve ballots from the count. But including these twelve, their recount came to exactly the same total as the poll commission had written on the protocol on the night of the election. A new set of protocols was written and signed by the poll commission members reflecting the corrected figures.

So for the time being it looked like poll 867 was off the table. However, we had heard earlier in the day that Raikovich's team would be moving on to a complaint about poll 852 the next day in the courts. So, final results were no nearer. With that, the District Election Commission members repackaged and resealed the counted ballots and put all the other packages back in the white bag unopened.

This is the point in the process that really surprised me and caused me to whisper to Matti. However, at least on the surface, everyone else in the room seems satisfied. Certainly, no one is looking forward to the prospect of the district commission holding up more than 1,600 unused ballots one by one for us to see. That would take all night.

We come out into the hall after 11:00 p.m. to find several women from poll 861's commission waiting in the cold corridor. We heard in the morning that Raikovich's team had filed a complaint at the City Election Commission about poll 861, citing various minor violations. But at the City Election Commission, Chairman Chaika had told Mikhail and Nino from ENEMO that he would not make a decision on this complaint and would forward it to the courts. The women from poll 861 now tell us that earlier in the evening – when every critical observer in the city was in the room with us at the Kirovska district commission – the City Election Commission had indeed ruled on the complaint, possibly the first complaint they had dealt during the whole electoral process. And they had come to the conclusion that the poll 861 votes should also be recounted by the district commission.

These commission members from poll 861 have been waiting through the whole recount of poll 867 and now they are being told to go home and come back again the next afternoon. We speak to one commission member, a feisty but frail eighty-four-year-old grandmother. A lock of snow-white hair is just visible under the floral babushka head scarf she has tied under her chin, and she has her large purse clutched firmly under her arm.

"We are ready for this recount," she declares. "I am going to protect the democratic rights of our voters!" I wonder how that recount will be conducted.

On the drive home I explain to Oksana how a recount is really supposed to work. "You have to count all the ballots. The ones that were used, and the ones left over. Otherwise, later someone can say that there could have been used ballots hidden with the unused ones, or with the spoiled ones. Or that some ballots were missing or had been added. If you don't account for every ballot issued to the poll, it leaves the whole recount open to the criticism that it was incomplete."

"So, you think it is a setup for another complaint?"

"Don't you?"

It is after midnight before Matti and I email another report to the core team. We are at the end of E-Day+2 and the City Election Commission has effectively refused to deal with the complaint about poll 861 and has sent it back to Kirovska district for a recount. And the district has found no errors in the 867 recount. Raikovich's team seems no closer to overturning the results, but Strizhakov's team is no closer to getting their win confirmed either.

V

18 November 2015, E-Day+3

By Wednesday, having failed to get any traction with the 867 recount at the District Election Commission, Raikovich's team is trying their hand at other levels. We are unable to observe, but we hear that during the day they tried to introduce new complaints about polls 863 and 864 at the City Election Commission. Without considering the substance of these complaints, the commission dismisses both for failing to meet the requirements of the law for the layout and contents of the complaint. It sounds like however much Chaika and Frosniak would like to see the BBPS candidate become mayor, the City Election Commission does not want to be seen to be party to spurious attempts to invalidate votes.

During the city's deliberations, we are tied up waiting to see Raikovich's team take their complaints about poll 852 to the Kirovohrad Administrative Court. We have waited the better part of the day by the time we shuffle our way in between the narrow benches, effectively becoming trapped in our seats. The rooms at the court are surprisingly small and seem to have been repurposed from hotel rooms. It's a tight squeeze to fit in us observers along with the lawyers, the representatives of the Raikovich team, the commission members from poll 852, and Deputy Chair Bezzubov from the Kirovska District Election Commission, not to mention the three judges, resplendent in their black robes. Oksana sits between Matti and me so that she can interpret quietly and not disturb the proceedings, which finally start at 3:30 in the afternoon.

The lawyer for Raikovich launches into his case claiming that on two of the protocols submitted by poll 852 to the District Election Commission on election night, there were ten letters of unclear handwriting. He doesn't dispute the number of votes though. Apparently, the poll members from 852 had been sent away to correct the handwriting errors and two corrected replacement protocols were brought back to the district commission and were accepted. Then, at some point later in the night, he alleges that the poll 852 commission had reconvened and created eighteen new protocols to replace the first set. This, the lawyer insists, was a major procedural error which called into question the poll's entire work.

The judges appear to be neutral and conscientious. They challenge Raikovich's lawyer to link this complaint to any of the criteria in the law for invalidating ballots. This is the first election I had observed where we were provided with an English copy of the Law on Local Elections, so I follow along as they discuss specific clauses. And I have to agree with the judges that the lawyer fails to explain how his complaint would lead to invalidating ballots under the law.

Next, witnesses from the poll testify. They point out that there was a shortage of blank protocols at the district that night, which is confirmed by Bezzubov. And, they add, it was people from Raikovich's headquarters who told them to make the extra protocols, not the District Election Commission.

At this point, Bezzubov backs down and suggests that perhaps a better resolution would be a recount. The judges point out that recounts are for the District Election Commission to decide, not the court, and then they adjourn to write their decision. It looks like Raikovich's case against poll commission 852 has fallen apart.

The story sounds all too familiar. Mirroring what happened to the poll 867 commission on election night, poll 852 was also subjected to rounds of unnecessary corrections to protocols. Each round of rewriting held the risk of actually introducing errors in the protocols rather than correcting them. That sounded to us like another strategy to set up the conditions to invalidate votes after an otherwise flawless voting process. The administrative court judges do not seem predisposed to participate in this sham.

It is nearly 6:00 p.m. when we get out of the court. Arriving at the Kirovska district office for the third evening in a row, we are surprised to find the room closed and a signed paper seal pasted across the joint between the doors. Raikovich's proxy is waiting outside along with City Election Commission Deputy Chair Oksana Frosniak, looking smug in her fur coat and high heels. They call up District Secretary Lokareva, who arrives and explains that Chaika, chair of the city commission, suggested that the district postpone the recount of poll 861 because Bezzubov was in court with us when the recount should have started. So Lokareva had closed and sealed the door at 5:30 p.m. and sent everyone home. Raikovich's proxy and Oksana are laughing between themselves at this turn of events, which we suspect puts the District Election Commission at risk of being accused of not being open and on the job. However, we are relieved that we don't have to sit through a recount after a long day at the court.

Oksana smirks as I take a photo of the handmade paper seal on the door. But it strikes me that, along with a key for the rickety door's lock, this strip of paper is all that is safeguarding the pile of seventy-four bags of ballots still waiting in the room for the final handover to the city commission. It wouldn't be difficult for someone to break into the room and remove a few bags and throw the whole district's votes into question.

However, it doesn't look like that is part of anyone's plan. Interfering with the votes of all of the polls would be so ... 2004. And the election officials in Kirovohrad are desperately trying to appear to have risen above the corruption of ten years ago. They want to keep everything within the law, short of recognizing the actual results of the election.

As it is, over the day we have collected gossip that suggests the narrative is subtly shifting. Internet chatter has returned to the idea that all along there had been an agreement between Strizhakov and Raikovich that Strizhakov should be Raikovich's deputy. Strizhakov was never meant to win, and his win – however narrow – was totally unexpected. Raikovich's team has been taken by surprise and doesn't know what to do. Strizhakov, it is said, is content to give up his victory, in exchange for whatever job and money he has been offered – and certainly, we observe he is doing nothing to defend his votes. For example, he did not send anyone to court to poke holes in the flimsy case presented by Raikovich's lawyer.

But Strizhakov's lead is genuine. At the end of E-Day+3, Raikovich's team has failed to make headway against poll 852 in the courts. The city commission has dismissed complaints about polls 863 and 864 without considering their substance. And the district commission has avoided dealing with complaints or recounting poll 861 by closing early. So, despite the continued search for a useable violation, Raikovich has failed to find any loophole which would invalidate a real victory. However, he has delayed for another day any declaration of a Strizhakov victory.

We cycle back through the court, hoping to get a copy of their decision, then the district to see if they have reopened, and finally the city commission to see if anything new has come up, before we go home to write what is now our daily report.

VI

19 November 2015, E-Day+4

Thursday morning, I take one of my last early morning walks through the streets of Kirovohrad, knowing that we will be leaving in two days. Walking past the offices of the City Election Commission, I look up at the third-floor windows of the commission offices where I see Secretary

Osadchiy looking out. I think he looks a bit forlorn, already in the office and probably wondering whether today would bring any solution to the electoral dilemma that is eating up the lives of so many commission members across the city. He raises his hand to me, probably thinking I am taking my observation job too far if I am coming by to check on his work at such an early hour. I return his wave and keep walking.

The weekly newspapers are out today, and our team convenes by 9:00 a.m. to review the coverage. In the absence of official results, both candidates have taken to the media to assert their win. On Tuesday night, Kirovohrad state TV, which heavily favoured Raikovich during the campaign, reported his campaign headquarters' claim of victory. And now we see that both sides have also placed paid advertorial in the papers giving their own numbers for the results. Ramping up the tension, Raikovich issues a statement alleging vote buying while Strizhakov threatens a slander court case in reply via Facebook.

We visit the district and city commissions again. As usual, I am a bit unsettled by the cheerful disdain that we receive from the city deputy chair, Oksana Frosniak. She seems to think our questions are either a waste of her time or a joke. Scrolling through our Kirovohrad contacts on Facebook later, I click through to Oksana's homepage and puzzle over her banner photo of an urban night sky.

"Where is that supposed to be?" I ask Oksana. "That's not Kyiv is it?"

She leans over my phone. "No, no. I think that's Washington."

"Oh, yeah, it's the Capitol. But why would she have a picture of Washington for her banner?"

"I think that comes from that American TV show, *House of Cards*."

"OMG!" it dawns on me. "Does she imagine she is a character out of *House of Cards*?" I can't decide whether to laugh or be aghast. Because in fact, that smug smile on Oksana's face does suggest that she is quite enjoying her current opportunity to emulate the Machiavellian manipulations that characterize White House politics on the hit Netflix series. Life imitates art indeed!

On our way out of the city commission offices, we meet Chairwoman Kirichenko from poll 867 on the stairs. She has just returned all her poll materials, including the all-important official stamp that is essential to making protocols and other official documents. She looks relieved that her part in the drama is nearly over, although there are still outstanding court proceedings. We are again impressed by her honesty and determination to resist the pressure to manipulate her poll's results.

With other potential manipulations before us in another evening recount, and given that my silent presence is all I have to offer, I decide I might benefit from looking more imposing as an observer. Professional Ukrainian women like the poll 867 chairwoman always dress well and good quality leather boots are often part of the outfit. Moreover, the temperature is falling as we are approaching the end of the third week of November. In the afternoon I go shopping for a pair of Ukrainian-made knee-high black leather boots and black tights. Wearing a black pencil skirt and the new boots, I feel ready to march back into action.

At 5:30, we settle in to another three hours of watching ballots held up at the district commission. The recount of poll 861 is identical to the recount of poll 867, with a slow deliberate perusal of each ballot and intense discussions about small ink marks at the edge of the odd ballot. Poll 861's chairwoman Zhabchik stands by throughout. She says little, but her defiant stance seems to dare the district commission to find anything wrong in how she conducted her poll. And, at the end of the count, poll 861's protocols are accepted by the district commission with very minor changes. At the end of the meeting Zhabchik comes up to Matti and me and thanks us for being there, saying she appreciates the support international observers provide in keeping things honest. I feel a little embarrassed as we are just doing our job and I have no idea whether our presence can keep anything honest in the long run.

Now the district commission has valid protocols for all seventy-four polls. However, the decision from the previous day's case at the Kirovohrad Administrative Court instructs the District Election Commission to wait for the court's further decisions before completing their combined results protocol. So, the deadlock continues.

By the end of E-Day+4, Raikovich has not persuaded the district commission to change or reject the results from any polls. He has continued to delay the results being released by appealing the case he lost against poll 867 at the Kirovska District Court to the Dnipropetrovsk Appellate

Court. While waiting for that decision, both candidates are appealing to the court of public opinion through the media. Everyone is looking towards the next day and the impending clash between the legal deadline that requires election commissions to produce results by midnight five days after the election and the court's instruction to hold off on producing results until the court decisions are final.

VII

20 November 2015, E-Day+5

We wake up Friday to a last full day of observations that promises to be dominated by court proceedings. When we get to the district commission at 10:30, we learn that they had already made a formal decision at 9:00 a.m. to hold off releasing results in keeping with the previous day's instructions from the administrative court. This decision has been sent to the Central Election Commission in Kyiv and, after discussions with Kyiv, the district commission feels that they have verbal approval to follow the court instructions to wait, rather than follow the law which says publish results by midnight. This seems quite significant, as the law is quite clear on the issue.

We also learn that, as we had predicted, the Raikovich team is now taking the District Election Commission to the Kirovohrad Administrative Court for failing to follow correct procedures during the recount of poll 867 on Tuesday. Raikovich is again insisting that the procedural errors should result in all of poll 867's votes being removed from the election count. They are not letting up!

After a false start at the courthouse at 11:30, the case finally opens at 4:00 p.m. in another cramped courtroom at the administrative court. It is a strange situation indeed. The district commission has sent Deputy Chair Bezzubov to represent them, as he is a lawyer. However, as he also represents Raikovich's party on the commission, he is in a serous conflict of interest, and it shows. His arguments are weak, and he readily agrees that his commission did not follow the correct procedures for a recount. The judges on the other hand seem quite ready to consider turning down Raikovich's complaint. They ask Bezzubov challenging questions and focus on the original weak grounds for the recount, rather than the flawed recount process.

After two hours of testimony, and knowing full well that the district commission is supposed to finalize their results by Friday midnight, the judges postpone hearing the balance of the case until 11:00 a.m. Saturday. The reason they give is that state TV has not provided their video of poll 867's recount, but it sounds to us like an excuse to avoid being perceived as the ones who determined the outcome of the election. They know that the decision from the Dnipropetrovsk Appellate Court on the other outstanding case against poll 867 could remove their responsibility for making this critical decision. We still haven't seen a copy of that ruling, but we hear that the appellate court declined to invalidate poll 867's ballots. However, they ruled that the poll commission must address the original complaints made on election night.

As the day draws to a close, we are even more convinced that the winning candidate, Strizhakov, doesn't actually want the mayor's job and is hoping that either an election commission or the courts will find some legal way to overturn his upset victory. We have noticed that he has not sent his proxies or lawyers to be party to, or observe, any of the court complaints or the poll 861 recount on Thursday. And none of his representatives are anywhere in sight tonight at the commissions. Apart from one statement to the media and some advertorial in Thursday's newspapers, Strizhakov has been surprisingly quiet this week and does not appear to be actively defending his lead in the votes, which has been under attack all week.

In a quiet moment checking the reactions on Facebook, I click through to the homepage of Strizhakov's wife. She has posted pictures of herself swimming with her kids somewhere very sunny. The post doesn't say where they are, but there is nowhere in Ukraine where you could enjoy an outside swim this late in November. It looks to me like his family is out of town somewhere warm – perhaps one of those resorts popular with Ukrainians on the Red Sea. Certainly not what you would expect from the spouse of a man about to celebrate his new job as the mayor.

We make our final visits to the City and District Election Commissions after 6:00 p.m. The court decision to delay the district results did not refer to the city commission. But Chairman Chaika points out to us they could hardly make the city results protocol without the Kirovska district results. So, both commissions are in a bind. We leave the members from each commission around 7:30 pm, sitting in their offices on either side of the main square in Kirovohrad, desperately paging through rumpled copies of the law trying to find some solution.

E-Day+5 ends with everything still up in the air. Raikovich's team has again failed to get a definitive decision out of the Kirovohrad Administrative Court about poll 867. They might have a partial win at the appeals court on poll 867, but the decision is not official yet. And with a countdown to the legal requirement for results to be published this midnight, the city and district commissions are unsure whether to follow court instructions to wait and ignore the law, or to follow legal requirement to publish and ignore the courts. There is no other way to describe their no-win situation but a mess.

VIII

21 November 2015, E-Day+6

I am up early Saturday, our last day in Kirovohrad, as I have to finish packing up the apartment that had been my temporary home for nine weeks. It is frustrating to have to deal with the practicalities of disposing household possessions acquired over two months and closing our temporary office when we know that the political process we are supposed to be observing is still going on. We rush through our logistics in time for our final in-person observations at the administrative court at 11:00 a.m.

Yet again we are trapped between the narrow benches as a boxy TV is rolled in so the judges can view the video of the poll 867 recount that the state TV channel had finally delivered. It is even more tedious to watch on video than it was in person, and after a while we begin to quietly question why they think they need to see the whole thing. Eventually we leave for our end-of-mission lunch with Oksana and Anton. Anton has been promising to take us to the "Hunter's Restaurant," which turns out to be decorated with the largest and most bizarre array of taxidermy you could imagine. It is an appropriate spot to end an observation mission that has involved so many surreal moments.

Even after we leave for Kyiv that afternoon, I can't get the ongoing crisis in Kirovohrad out of my mind. Oksana calls us on the train with updates. She has found out that while we had been tied up at the court, the City Election Commission had agreed with a request from Raikovich to change all eight of his members of poll commission 867, including Kirichenko who we had last seen at the city offices Thursday. Presumably Raikovich's team has decided that none of these commission members can be relied on to bow to pressure.

This city decision is clearly outside the law, which states in Article 23.8 that the latest date for changing members of a poll commission is the day before voting.[2] However, the city commission acquiesced to Raikovich's request, probably because it will effectively push any decision about invalidating ballots off their table and back to poll 867. We now question if it was a coincidence that they came up with this compromise while we were conveniently stuck observing that video at the court.

As our train rolls across the dark countryside towards Kyiv, a session of the reconstituted poll 867 commission is convened. They meet in a crowded schoolroom with the members crammed into small student desks. Chairwoman Kirichenko has been removed from the commission and the new chair lectures them like a schoolteacher from the front of the class. They are presented with a resolution prepared in advance that responds to the instructions of the Dnipropetrovsk Appellate Court that the poll commission must rule on the complaints made on election night. The resolution frames a decision that would invalidate all the votes in the poll in response to the complaint that people not on the voters list had put ballots in the box (e.g., children who dropped in their parent's ballots.) Secretary Olga Zeifert, representing Strizhakov, stands. The strain of the week is showing, and she has a toque pulled over her hair and her hands thrust in her jacket pockets. She tells the new commission members that what they are trying to do is not right before she leads the Strizhakov commission members off to complain to the city commission, leaving the poll commission without a quorum. Journalists from the local online media capture the whole argument on video and post a link to YouTube along with their article.[3] As E-Day+6 draws to a close, Raikovich still has not changed the results in his favour, but there is no hiding what is going on.

IX

22 November 2015, E-Day+7

Now we come full circle to the story which began this book. Sunday, while we attend the final long-term observer debriefing in Kyiv, the City Election Commission finally creates the conditions to ensure Raikovich's win. We learn from online news sites that after the failure of the Saturday meeting at poll 867, on Sunday the City Election Commission removes two key supporters of Strizhakov from the poll 867 commission. For the temerity of challenging the legitimacy of the replacement BPPS commission members, Secretary Olga Zeifert and commission member Tetyana Melnychenko are dismissed, ostensibly for "sabotaging" the poll commission meeting.[4]

A new meeting of poll 867 is called Sunday evening. This is the point where the Strizhakov commission member makes her call to me in Kyiv while the Strizhakov supporters are caucusing outside on the steps of the school. When they know no one else is coming to see what is happening, five commission members supporting Strizhakov return to the meeting. The new compliant Raikovich supporters are in a majority and with little ado these new members – who had not even been in the poll on election day – vote to invalidate all the ballots from poll 867. Something similar occurs with poll 861. We don't learn the details, but it likely involves one of the complaints filed by the Frosniak brothers a week ago. And with that, E-Day+7 concludes with the Raikovich team finally succeeding to remove enough votes from the count to tip the balance in their favour.

X

23 November 2015, E-Day+8

Monday is our last day in the country, but we are still observing what the alternative press is reporting online. The reporter from the Gret4ka online news site is in the City Election Commission offices at 8:00 a.m. as the commission finally prepares its combined results protocols, giving Raikovich a lead of 378 votes over Strizhakov.[5]

In the accompanying photos, Chairman Chaika looks tired and resigned. Secretary Osadchiy, identified as one of only two commission members who voted against the decision on the results, is sitting at his computer at the back of the room looking disappointed, isolated, and disenchanted. And Deputy Oksana Frosniak is pictured signing protocols with a smug grin on her face, clearly delighted to have ended the electoral process on the winning team after all.[6]

It is frustrating not to be able to observe in person through to the end. But it is encouraging to see that local civil society observers and online news sites are all there and publishing consistent accounts of what happened. The scandal is completely public. We file our final report to the core team before we leave for the airport. Our mission is over, and it is time for us to move on.

11   Conclusions

I

The whole point of an election observation mission is to publicly report what has been seen. So the release of the mission reports is very important. The standard approach is to produce a short press release (one to two pages) and a longer preliminary statement (about ten pages) quickly after election day. The hope is that the findings of the mission, based on a large number of neutral observations collected before and during the vote, can provide an honest assessment and combat any misinformation that may be flying around about what happened on election day. However, there are trade-offs when the preliminary statement is released before the full outcome of the election is known.[1]

The preliminary statement is always followed by a more detailed final report, but that final report doesn't come out for a couple of months. By then most people have lost interest. So despite the fact that it is a very early summary of what happened, the preliminary statement is the most influential document, and the first couple of pages that comprise the executive summary are the most read part. If those key pages give a rosier picture – or can be interpreted as a rosier picture – than the more detailed report, that will be what is remembered.[2] We came up against this problem frequently when I observed presidential elections in Osh, Kyrgyzstan, in 2011.

"Why do your OSCE reports always say that our elections are good when we know they are bad?" Gulgaky demanded to know. Compiling and publishing written reports is the primary way that election observers communicate their findings, but it is surprising how often what is written down in black and white comes across as gray and murky.

Gulgaky, a local NGO leader, was a feisty and frank woman and she didn't pull her punches. I was initially taken aback. On my previous mission in Ukraine, all of the people we met were respectful and many thanked us for the work of international observers. But it sounded like some Kyrgyz had a very different experience of the OSCE's work. Gulgaky was annoyed, and she wanted us to know it.

I couldn't help but respond defensively. "In fact," I countered, "OSCE reports have been quite critical of elections in Kyrgyzstan."

"That's not what we hear on the television. When our politicians get elected, they always tell us that the OSCE said their election was all good. But I have been observing in our election polls for years. We know that every member of the poll staff can be bought, and my organization has documented all kinds of falsifications."

Gulgaky's NGO was a well-respected local organization that had years of experience monitoring local human rights, including elections, and I couldn't dispute their observations.

"Have you taken any complaints to the courts?" I asked.

"What's the point?" she replied. "The Justice Department works for the government. The district election officials cheat openly in front of our observers. They know there is nothing we can do about it."

"So, what do you do?"

"We report our observations to the media and on our website. We don't sit quiet!"

In the following weeks we heard these concerns repeated multiple times. People spontaneously told us that OSCE reports said that Kyrgyz elections were good, but they knew otherwise.

When we asked, it turned out that few people in our area had actually read any of our reports, even though they were translated into Kyrgyz and Russian. When I read through OSCE reports from previous elections in Kyrgyzstan I could see why. Election monitoring reports are often long, and the full conclusions are buried in diplomatic language that requires reading between the lines and persistence to get to the end of the report.[3]

Sadly, the report produced for this election turned out to be no better. The preliminary statement released the day after the election opened with the obscure suggestion that "shortcomings underscored that the integrity of the electoral process should be improved to consolidate democratic practice in line with international commitments."

However, the tiny minority of readers who made it through to the tenth page would have found that the shortcomings OSCE observers like our team had concerns with included "ballot box stuffing, multiple and family voting, vote buying, and bussing of voters" along with "unauthorized persons in polling stations" and "poor quality voters lists." We saw that "the process worsened during the counting" and "further deteriorated during the tabulation." And we knew that these things had to improve if the government was going "to build confidence in the integrity of the vote."

But the reality was that the only thing that the average Kyrgyz voter would have heard was the losing opposition candidate who stood up during the live telecast of the OSCE press conference and accused the organization of yet again endorsing a corrupt process.

As my partner and I complained in our final report to the core team, and reiterated in person during the final debriefing, "If the OSCE/ODIHR has this much difficulty communicating its message, it raises the question of why we continue to monitor elections [in Kyrgyzstan]. It is counterproductive if our findings are misconstrued and manipulated by local politicians. If politicians are able to pass the blame for corruption onto the OSCE/ODIHR there is a big problem with communication."

II

It is almost as bad to see a mission's findings ignored as it is to see them misconstrued. The preliminary statement that comes out the day after the second round of voting in the Ukrainian local elections in 2015 has nothing specific to say about Kirovohrad because the results are still up in the air and the OSCE's observations get no local attention. The final report that is released in February 2016 includes an accurate, if short, description of how the results of the Kirovohrad mayor's election were overturned. However, most other mayor's races concluded without serious irregularities. And the Kirovohrad race is not the most problematic in the country. The race for mayor of Kryvyi Rih is still mired in controversy three months after voting day.

Meanwhile in Kirovohrad, Raikovich is already firmly ensconced in the mayor's chair and Strizhakov has lost his final court challenge of the results and moved on to other things. It isn't how Raikovich wanted to win, and it isn't how Strizhakov wanted to lose, so no one is really happy, except perhaps people like the Frosniaks, who live for the thrill of the game. But the election is already old news in Kirovohrad and the OSCE report makes no waves before it slips quietly beneath the water.

III

What conclusions can I draw from the story of the Kirovohrad election, and the other elections I observed? Do international election observers make a difference? Does our work really matter?

The first lesson is that building trust in electoral processes is slow and takes many years. When citizens and political actors don't trust the electoral system, they are more likely to game it and fulfill their own prophesies about interference. However, trust – or lack of trust – in the electoral system cannot be separated from trust in the broader systems and institutions in society. A 2020 survey found that more than three quarters of Ukrainians did not trust their judicial system or their state apparatus and about 70 per cent did not trust political parties. The few institutions that the majority did trust were the armed forces, volunteer battalions, the church, and volunteer organizations.[4] This lack of trust ties in with the reality many Ukrainians perceive – or have actually experienced – that their political parties and state institutions, including the courts, are corrupt and are weak at protecting the interests of ordinary citizens. In 2021, Transparency International ranked Ukraine in the bottom third on its Corruption Perceptions Index.[5] Electoral corruption is just another example of the day-to-day corruption many Ukrainians experience, especially small businesspeople, as we realized in Dnipropetrovsk in 2012 at the end of the parliamentary elections.

"Our main service is a 'flying squad' of lawyers who support our members." The representative of the Small and Medium Business Support Association paused to sip from his coffee. Voting in the election was over and our final report had been submitted that morning. But the association had finally responded to our request for a meeting, and we felt we should listen to what they had to say, even if we were late talking with them.

"So, what does this 'flying squad' do?" Bart asked. I was imagining that lawyers might help with interpreting the law, perhaps finessing the notoriously complex tax code, or maybe walking through the requirements of municipal regulations. Things like that. I was way off base.

"When the heavies from the local organized crime boss arrive to demand protection money, our members can call in these lawyers. Our lawyers are good at helping negotiate the lowest payments a business can get away with. It's hard for our small members to deal with these criminals alone. Crime bosses have a lot of power in this city."

Their description was a wake-up call for Bart and me. This election, which had been so central to our time in Dnipropetrovsk, was just a passing battle between the local oligarchs, far above the heads of ordinary people. Small business owners were faced with street-level pressures that were only tangentially connected to electoral politics. In the local market, men with guns turning up and demanding money to let you remain in business made casting a ballot seem of minimal importance.

Our driver was one of these small businessmen. Along with the car we drove in, he owned a half-container truck and a twenty-seat bus. When I asked him if he had aspirations to expand his transport business, he was evasive.

"Well, if I got any bigger, I would attract the attention of powerful people," he explained. "It's probably better for me to stay small enough to fly below their radar." It made sense for him on a personal level, but it was a sad example of how organized crime and corruption were putting significant brakes on economic growth across Ukraine.

Election monitoring cannot fix problems like that. On the contrary, when election observers accurately report on corruption in electoral processes, we feed into those broader perceptions and mistrust. That's not a reason to stop observing, but it is a reason to temper expectations.

If you hope to see an immediate impact and large-scale change at the national level as a result of election monitoring and reporting, I suspect you will often be disappointed. The evidence suggests that kind of change rarely happens. Academics who have analyzed the cumulative impact of election observation over multiple missions suggest that monitoring may increase the domestic cost of cheating and encourage the reform of election laws and practices, but most change is slow and there can be as many steps backwards as forwards.[6]

There have been a few examples of immediate change. Perhaps the most famous example was the rerun of the presidential election during the Orange Revolution in Ukraine in 2004. In the presence of large numbers of local and international observers, the Ukrainian people demonstrated that they could run a much better electoral process within a few weeks of a very flawed election. As the OSCE concluded, improvements during the rerun election were "in stark contrast to the previous votes, and demonstrate that when a clear political will is evident to conduct an election in line with OSCE commitments, much can ultimately be achieved in a short time period."[7] However, it took five more years before Ukraine fully implemented the unified State Register of Voters, which addressed the problems of inadequate voters lists that plagued the 2004 election. And not all subsequent Ukrainian elections have received the glowing review of the 2004 rerun vote.

IV

Secondly, the impact of international election monitoring is limited by a lack of international mechanisms to enforce recommendations. Observers can only shine a light on shortcomings and encourage change. For international monitoring and reporting on democracy at the national level to have a real impact, there must be sanctions available to major international actors, and they have to be prepared to exercise those sanctions. In practice, broader geopolitical considerations often trump any desire to directly punish undemocratic leaders.

For example, following the 2006 presidential vote in Tajikistan, the OSCE condemned the election because, as we had seen, the race was "characterized by a marked absence of competition" and "voters were presented with a choice that was only nominal."[8] Yet the Canadian government, along with other major bilateral and multilateral donors, continued to provide foreign aid that propped up a president who showed no interest in democratic competition and continued to line his pockets at the expense of his already impoverished people. The truth was that the donors were primarily interested in the stability of this remote central Asian republic that bordered on troubled Afghanistan, where donor countries were mired in an unwinnable counter-insurgency operation.

In 2007, President Nazarbaev of Kazakhstan was actively lobbying for the rotating chairmanship of the OSCE when we monitored parliamentary elections and I collected concrete evidence of vote stealing and the falsification of results. My work contributed to the final conclusions of our OSCE mission that "the election did not meet a number of OSCE commitments, in particular with regard to ... the vote count and tabulation."[9] Despite these reports, Kazakhstan was awarded the chairmanship of the OSCE in 2010 and got the prestige that went with it. OSCE member countries needed an olive branch to reach out to the former Soviet republics who felt the organization did not respect their situation and, despite his corrupt elections, Nazarbaev was the beneficiary of that gesture.[10]

As my airplane taxied into Manas International Airport in Kyrgyzstan in 2010, one of the first impressions I got through the window was a long line of hulking grey C130 military transport planes parked along the runway apron. The Americans were paying a steep rent to maintain a military facility at the airport to transit NATO personnel and material in and out of Afghanistan. At the same time the Russians had their own base about twenty kilometres away, concrete evidence that the Kyrgyz government was engaged in a complex strategic game playing off the two superpowers. The OSCE's negative assessment of the 2010 election would have no discernible impact on the continued investment of either of these countries in Kyrgyzstan, nor did it deter private Canadian investment in the Kumtor gold mine that was a major contributor to GDP.

If rapid democratic change at the national level is your definition of success, then election monitoring and reporting has serious limitations for achieving that goal. Expecting a country to significantly change how it runs elections, even after repeated missions and recommendations, is unrealistic. Parties and politicians will continue to game the system. Dictators will hold on to power. And, despite their rhetoric about promoting democracy, the powerful international actors have other things on their minds. It's depressing but true.

V

Thirdly, strong observation during the voting process doesn't so much prevent manipulation as influence where the interference takes place. Consistent monitoring around election day may make it more difficult to steal the votes during voting, counting at the polls, and during tabulation. But that may just push manipulation away from the ballot box and into the courts where cases attempting to invalidate the votes can be drawn out until observers are no longer around and backroom pressure on judges is harder to see. That is not only bad for the election, but it contributes to wider mistrust in the judiciary.[11] Strong election day monitoring may also encourage politicians to try to buy the votes in the pre-election period before most observers are on the job. It may also drive powerful figures to take control of the media so they can prepare the field for their preferred candidates. It is difficult to prove the impact of media ownership on election coverage or to prove the impact of election coverage on actual votes, so the media can be a safer space for manipulating the electorate than directly at the ballot box. Powerful political figures in Kirovohrad did own local newspapers, but there was no way we could measure how much they influenced voters.

VI

A fourth lesson was that voters aren't the only ones being manipulated. Although international observers can help to provide a neutral overview of a contested election, they can be at risk of being played as tools in a political strategy to undermine confidence in the election results. When all sides are using the same techniques for cheating and alleging cheating, it can be very difficult to determine what is true, and how much cheating affected the vote.[12] I interviewed many local political actors in Ukraine who threw around allegations about falsification without concrete evidence, hoping that we international observers would give the accusations credence and repeat them. I suspect they hoped to exploit our apparent lack of experience and naivety (rarely true), or even play on some observers' secret wish to score personal points by spotting corruption. No doubt, some local actors were genuinely afraid that meddling would occur. But others knew they were not going to be on the winning side and were tossing sand in the observers' eyes to make their opponent's victory questionable. The OSCE methodology – such as always sending observers in pairs, always from a different country, and usually a man and a woman, and looking for verification if not hard evidence wherever possible – reduces the chances that observers will fall for false allegations.

VII

A more encouraging fifth lesson was that local observers are actively participating in the democratic process. International observers may find it difficult to sort out fact from fiction in a foreign country. Local observers, including alternative media, are more likely to have a good sense of what is going on, and they are increasingly talking about what they see. There were many observers, partisan and non-partisan, in the polls I visited in Ukraine. In Kharkiv in 2010, during the first presidential elections after the rerun of the 2004 elections, many polls had more than fifteen observers in them on election day. These observers didn't often have much to say, but they were there, watching and upping the ante for anyone considering stealing the votes.

By the time we observed in Kirovohrad five years later, the smart phone had arrived and more and more of what local observers were seeing during elections was available online. There were few secrets about the Kirovohrad election, then and now. Local observers and the alternative press saw what we saw in the commission meetings and the courts and more, and they posted what they saw online. And much of it was still online in 2023. The smart phone and the internet are making it much harder to hide electoral corruption and it is local observers who are using those tools most effectively.

VIII

Finally, as we saw at the local level, long-term and short-term international observers, by their presence and their respectful interaction with the people on the ground, can help support and build the confidence of people involved in electoral politics. When observers meet with individuals, they demonstrate respect for what those people are doing. When international observers listen to local people's stories and report what they have to say, they show local actors that what they are doing is part of a bigger democratic movement to help everyone everywhere have their vote, get it counted, and see their chosen representatives in government.

I still wonder if it would have made a difference to the outcome of the mayor's election if Matti and I had been there to observe the final machinations. Were the local political players in Kirovohrad really concerned about what the international observers saw and what we said about it? Would the members of the City Election Commission have been too embarrassed to change the poll commission members in violation of the election law if we had been sitting in that classroom on Dvortsova Street watching them? Had they somehow engineered the extended court sitting on Saturday morning to keep us tied up until they had finished this distasteful business? Perhaps. After all, it was hard to believe that it was a coincidence that the City Election Commission made their earlier ruling that led to the recount of poll 861 when they knew all the observers – international, local, and media – were tied up watching the recount of poll 867. If they could avoid the glare of the public eye, they would. They knew we would be leaving eventually so in any case they could have waited us out.

But would our presence have made a difference to the women commission members at poll 867 if we had been there at the end, that Sunday night when they called me at my hotel in Kyiv? I think it would. The closer you get to the ground, the greater the power of an international presence. It might not have changed the outcome, but our presence would have validated their conviction that what was happening was not right, and that they had not made mistakes on election night. Making an impact on local people on a personal level is possible, valuable, and over the long-term may contribute to creating an environment that supports democratic human rights.

Perhaps the big national stories are not all important; perhaps it's the smaller human stories that matter. Which is why that phone call in the night was so disappointing. Because we couldn't do that small thing at the end. Our failure wasn't that we couldn't prevent the overturning of the election results. That was never within our power, or indeed our responsibility. Our failure was that we couldn't stand by that poll chairwoman and her colleagues to the end, and bear witness as her rights, and the rights of her voters, were trampled on. If we had been there a couple of days longer, we could have done that. But it wasn't to be.

All missions come to an end at some point. We international observers have to go home and get back to our day-to-day lives just as the local political actors and the election administrators have to hang up their election hats. We all have to get back to our day jobs, at least until another election comes around, and the cycle to prepare the field, win the votes, buy the votes, steal the votes, or invalidate the votes begins all over again.

Epilogue

Before I left Ukraine in 2015, Oksana suggested I might like to watch the new comedy series launched by the *Kvartal 95* studio, *Servant of the People*, where Volodymyr Zelensky played a schoolteacher who is improbably elected president. When I got home, I watched the whole first season on YouTube. The premier had English subtitles, but after that I was on my own practicing my Russian comprehension, but the premise was easy to follow. The plot revolved around Zelensky and his honest friends taking on corruption at the highest levels in the Ukrainian government. It was a light fantasy that kept me smiling warmly during a cold Canadian winter and pondering my experiences in Ukraine.

Back in Kirovohrad, the new local government administration took shape. With Raikovich firmly in the mayor's chair, Tabalov got the position of secretary of the city council. For their hard work managing the complaints process and ensuring that BPPS captured the mayor's office, Ruslan Frosniak got the position of head of the Leninski district council, while his friend Olexander Krishko snagged head of Kirovska district council, cementing the BPPS party's hold across municipal government in the city.

Reluctant to follow the results of the city name referendum and rename Kirovohrad with the Russian-flavoured name of Yelisavetgrad, Raikovich's council passed the problem of renaming the city up to the national level where the National Parliament decided to rename the city after the Ukrainian thespian, Kropyvnytskyi.

In 2016, I took a full-time job as a policy analyst, which was good for my bank account, but precluded extended time off to observe elections. I was very frustrated when I heard at the end of 2018 that Zelensky had announced that he was running for president. That would have been such an interesting race to observe! But I could only look on from afar.

I emailed my old interpreter Pavlo to find out what Ukrainians were thinking about Zelensky as a candidate. Pavlo, who was working for a team of election observers once again, framed his response in terms of the disappointment his friends felt with the rule of oligarchs.

"We all knew that [Poroshenko] is an oligarch and we all thought that he has enough money so there is no need for him to make more," he wrote. "We hoped that he would sacrifice himself and would really fight against corruption and would stop the war." And yet, he observed, "the war is still going on, [and] nobody from [Parliament] who is stealing money was prosecuted and went to jail."

In contrast, Pavlo saw Zelensky as a refreshing alternative. "Zelensky is not a member of this system, he is not a politician, his business is not connected with the Ukrainian budget, he didn't make money [with] the help of the government. He is an actor with strong managerial skills. A lot of people are afraid to vote for him at these elections because they do not know what to expect from him … Zelensky is a [comedian] who doesn't have any experience in politics but [he] wants to fight the system and change something in this country. So, who knows, maybe this is what we need right now."

Zelensky ran an innovative campaign, substituting his comedy shows for traditional political rallies and relying heavily on social media outreach.[1] Four months later, a large majority of Ukrainian voters agreed with Pavlo that this was the kind of change they wanted to see. Zelensky won the April 2019 elections with 73 per cent of the vote, by far the biggest victory margin of any president since the independence of Ukraine in 1991. The secretary of the Kropyvnytskyi City Election Commission representing Zelensky for the round two vote was Oksana Frosniak.[2] Ever the opportunists, the Frosniaks had abandoned Poroshenko's team and landed on the winning side again. During parliamentary elections in July 2019, Zelensky's Servant of the People Party went on to win the first single-party majority in the Ukrainian Parliament since independence.

The October 2020 local elections in Kirovohrad were a rematch between Raikovich and Strizhakov, who faced off against each other in a second round of voting again. However, this time Raikovich won convincingly. The scandal of the 2015 election was not forgotten, but it didn't seem to have had a negative impact on Raikovich's popularity.[3]

On 24 February 2022, my heart went out to all my friends in Ukraine when I learned that the Russians had begun their long-predicted invasion. On 7 March 2022, Zelensky promoted Mayor Raikovich to head of regional state administration to shore up the region's defences in the centre of the country.

By the end of 2022, as the Russian invasion of Ukraine approached its one-year anniversary, Ukrainians were being touted as the new great defenders of democracy.[4] For a country that Transparency International ranked 122 out of 180 countries in 2021 for public sector corruption, this might seem a bit ironic.[5] But reality is always more complex than a numbered ranking can capture. Over two decades observing Ukrainians politics, I have seen the hopes of Ukrainian voters rising and falling like children on a teeter totter, swinging between believing and doubting in the potential for a just democratic dispensation of power in their country. But drawing on a century of dreams of building an independent Ukrainian republic, many hang on to the belief that they can make democracy eventually work.

I hadn't planned to write about what I witnessed in Ukraine, but when the invasion began in earnest, I felt the time had come to share my experiences in the country. The invasion is a threat to democracy of a whole different order, and the whole world is now observing. It remains to be seen whether Ukraine will be able to hold regular elections in the foreseeable future. While I wait to see how the war unfolds, my memories of my election missions remain vivid, grounded as they are in powerful human exchanges and strong friendships with the ordinary people I met in Ukraine.

Acknowledgments

The things I learned about elections that enabled me to write this book, I did not learn alone. So, first and foremost, I must thank the members of all the long-term observer teams I served with. We went out together, day after day, to gather information and build an understanding of what was happening in each election we observed, and in elections in general.

In particular, our local assistants and drivers opened a window into their culture and society that was invaluable, and they worked tirelessly to get us closer to some version of the truth on the ground. In addition, I had the support of many dedicated core team members who worked into the night hours, advising and guiding our work in the field, and respectfully synthesizing and integrating our observations into the national reports that we can still read online. And of course, I must thank all the local people we interviewed and observed, who – for the most part – were generous with their time and information about the progress of their elections.

I also want to thank the team at CANADEM for giving me the privilege of representing Canada on seven long-term observer missions, and Global Affairs Canada for funding this important work.

Most importantly, I have to thank my fellow long-term observers. It is almost inevitable that you become close with your long-term observer partner after spending so many hours chatting in the back of the car during out-of-this-world field trips. Pulling up beside a roadside stand to buy buckets of fresh apples, and then tossing the cores out the window as you roll across the plains of central Asia. Zigzagging up vertiginous mountain passes and stopping for cigarettes and photos of snow-capped peaks from the summit before descending to the dusty plain below. Driving across the frozen Ukrainian steppes, watching the snow drift across vast fields between the treed windbreaks that disappear over the horizon. And after shared adventures and meals stretched out with anecdotes and reminiscences you become not far removed from an "old married couple," as the joke goes, or a brother and sister.

And yet you know you are unlikely to work together again once the mission is over. So when you find yourselves comparing notes and composing reports late in the evening, giddy with exhaustion, conspiratorial moments arise. Eventually, these men volunteer quiet truths about their personal lives: the divorce, the young second wife with the unexpected toddler, the ill-advised affair, the unlikely friendship with a prostitute, the uncertain girlfriend, the strained relations with children, the parent irrevocably slipping into dementia. The many variants of the human condition that can be interwoven with a life punctuated by months away from home on international missions. Confessions freely given, with no demand for similar tales in return. But these stories are never to be divulged, especially not in a book like this.

When I decided to write down the things that are appropriate to share, I was encouraged by friends and family in Canada and overseas. Colleagues from the world of election observation provided useful criticism of early drafts, particularly Ted Loiko, Chris Bassel, Stefan Krause, Christine Vincent, and Matti Heinonen. Other readers who gave helpful suggestions include Victoria Vanderlinden, Margaret Godoy, Sophia Bucking, and Sarah Cooper Godoy.

Finally, I am grateful to the team at MQUP who took my manuscript seriously enough to put it in your hands, including Jane Errington, Richard Ratzlaff, Jared Toney, and Katheen Fraser.

Appendix

Kirovohrad Mayoral Election Results, 2015

Table A.1 Round one results, Kirovohrad mayor's election, 25 October 2015

Candidate	Votes	%	Nominating party	Biography
Raikovich, Andrei	22,237	27%	BPPS and Fatherland Party	59, not a party member, general director of Yatran meat processing plant, deputy in the previous and current Oblast Rada.
Strizhakov, Artyom	19,917	25%	Self-nominated	31, no party, self-employed, deputy in previous city council.
Tabalov, Andrei	16,147	20%	Our Hometown Party	37, no party, general director of Big Fields dairy products company.
Atamanchuk, Vita	4,425	5%	Self-nominated	39, No party, deputy to the head of Kirovohrad Oblast State Administration (governor), only woman in the race, supported by organization of IDPs and ATO veterans.
Leybenko, Andrei	3,847	5%	Opposition Bloc	32, director of Pronto Group (a call centre), previously ran the Governor's Hot Line call centre under Sergei Larin.
Mickalonok, Sergei	2,907	4%	People's Control Party	49, party member, deputy director of private enterprise Kirovohradinvestbud.
Sanasaryan, Rafael	2,692	3%	Radical Party Oleg Lyashko	32, party member, director of Eurotechica-2007.
Kapitanov, Sergei	2,683	3%	Freedom Party	45, party member, retired militia officer, new to politics.
Rashupko, Vasil	2,285	3%	UKROP	31, party member, private entrepreneur.

Table A.1 Round one results, Kirovohrad mayor's election, 25 October 2015 *(continued)*

Candidate	Votes	%	Nominating party	Biography
Pusakov, Volodymir	2,148	3%	Self-nominated	66, no party, unemployed, previously mayor of the city.
Maksiuta, Andrei	523	1%	Self-nominated	32, no party, director of Falcon Security and Legal Firm.
Drobin, Andrei	494	1%	Self-nominated	39, party member, Socialist Party.
Borshulyak, Olexandar	487	1%	Self-nominated	59, no party, self-employed.
Obrezha, Volodymir	176	0%	Self-nominated	40, no party, general director of Deal Group.
Voted	80,968			
Did not vote	110,692			

Table A.2 Round two results, Kirovohrad mayor's election, 15 November 2015

Candidate	Nominating party	November 15 parallel count[1]	November 16 journalist's report[2]	November 23 City Election Commission final decision[3]
Raikovich, Andrei	BPPS and Fatherland Party	24,876	24,814	24,435
Strizhakov, Artyom	Self-nominated	25,272	25,069	24,057
Total votes		50,148	49,883	48,492
Raikovich's position		-396	-255	378

1 Depo.Kirovohrad, "U Stryzhakova Zaiavyly."
2 Dubyna, "Staly Vidomi Poperedni Rezul'taty."
3 Lebid, "U Kirovohradi Ofitsiino Oholosyly Rezul'taty Vyboriv Mis'koho Holovy."

Notes

INTRODUCTION

1 Fukuyama, "More Proof That This Really Is the End of History."
2 Repucci and Slipowitz, "Freedom in the World 2022."
3 Boese et al., "Democracy Report 2022."
4 Association of Municipalities of Ontario, "Ontario Municipal Elections."
5 CIDA, "Evaluation of CIDA's Ukraine Program"; Global Affairs Canada, "Evaluation of START and GPSF."
6 In Canada we call the district level a riding.

CHAPTER ONE – IT'S NOT OVER UNTIL IT'S OVER

1 Williams and Picarelli, "Organized Crime in Ukraine."
2 Collins, "Ireland's Voting System."
3 Woodward and Bernstein, *All the President's Men*.
4 Statistics Canada, "Voter Turnout Rates."
5 Association of Municipalities of Ontario, "Ontario Municipal Elections."

CHAPTER TWO – ASSEMBLING THE TEAM

1 CANADEM, "Democracy Promotion and Election Observation"; Global Affairs Canada, "Canada's Engagement in Ukraine."
2 Statistics Canada, "Census in Brief."
3 Bjornlund, *Beyond Free and Fair*, 129.
4 Hyde, *The Pseudo-Democrat's Dilemma*, 166.
5 The city of Kirovohrad was renamed Kropyvnytskyi in 2016 but the region is still called Kirovohrad.

CHAPTER THREE – PREPARE THE FIELD

1 Hudson Institute, "Ukraine's Rectification of Names."
2 Romaniuk and Gladun, "Demographic Trends in Ukraine," 321.
3 Worldometer, "Ukraine Population (2022)."
4 Notably, there is no Elections USA. Voting for the president takes place through fifty-two state elections (this includes Washington, DC, and Puerto Rico).
5 Snyder, *Bloodlands*, 81.

6 Clarity-project.info; opendatabot.ua; Trebunsky, "Vyborchi Komisiï."
7 OSCE/ODIHR, "Ukraine Early Presidential Elections 25 May 2014," 10.
8 OSCE/ODIHR, "Ukraine Local Elections, 25 October and 15 November 2015," 10.
9 OSCE/ODIHR, "Ukraine Presidential Election 31 October, 21 November, and 26 December 2004."
10 Uggen, "Locked Out 2020," 4.
11 CBC News, "All Prisoners Have the Right to Vote."
12 Didenko, "Ukrainian Guantanamo."
13 OSCE/ODIHR, "Ukraine Parliamentary Elections 28 October 2012," 28.
14 CBC News, "Elections Canada Working with Local Charities."
15 Opening Doors, "100,000 Children in Ukraine."
16 ReliefWeb, "Ukraine IDP Figures Analysis."
17 OSCE/ODIHR, "Ukraine Early Parliamentary Elections 26 October 2014," 13.
18 IOM, "IOM's Assistant."
19 OSCE/ODIHR, "Republic of Tajikistan," 1.
20 Käihkö, "A Nation-in-the-Making."
21 Eventually he will be immortalized in bronze in this same park.
22 Chesno, "Tymoshenko IUriĭ Volodymyrovych."

CHAPTER FOUR - WIN THE VOTES: ROUND ONE

1 OSCE/ODIHR, *Handbook for Long-Term Election Observers.*
2 Likhachev, "The 'Right Sector' and Others."
3 Yakovenko et al., "A Sticky Situation for Poroshenko."
4 Szostek, "Nothing Is True?"
5 *Vecherniĭ Kvartal Ot 19.10.2012.*
6 Golosnoy, "Who Is Maxim Golosnoy?"
7 In 2021 the OSCE will issue a special handbook to help international monitors observe campaigns on social networks, but in 2015 we were still making it up as we went along.
8 Likhachev, "The 'Right Sector' and Others."
9 Ibid.
10 Ibid.
11 Central Election Commission, "TSentral'na Vyborcha Komisiĭa Ukraïny."
12 Trishyna, "Vidterminovanyĭ Revansh: Stryzhakov."

CHAPTER FIVE - BUY THE VOTES

1 Balmforth, "For Sale on Internet."
2 Scrutton and Shah, *The Global State of Democracy 2022.*
3 Gee, "Doug Ford Sent Me a $440 Licence Plate Renewal Refund."
4 Ferguson, "Ford Government Offers Ontario Nurses a $5K 'Retention' Bonus."
5 OSCE/ODIHR, "Ukraine Local Elections, 25 October and 15 November 2015," 16.

CHAPTER SIX – STEAL THE VOTES

1 The osce now has an online course for observers, but that was not available in 2015. Individual participating states have always been responsible for training their own observers.
2 Snyder, *Bloodlands*, 215.
3 "2020 Belarussian Presidential Election."
4 OSCE/ODIHR, "Republic of Belarus."
5 Bjornlund, *Beyond Free and Fair*, 150.
6 Snyder, *Bloodlands*, 105.
7 This was the last election I covered without a digital camera, which greatly simplifies the process of copying documents.
8 Shevel, "The Repeat Second Round."
9 OSCE/ODIHR, "Ukraine Presidential Election 31 October, 21 November, and 26 December 2004."
10 Shevel, "The Repeat Second Round."

CHAPTER EIGHT – WIN THE VOTES AGAIN: ROUND TWO

1 See appendix for the full results of round one voting.
2 Talant, "Savik Shuster Returns as TV Host after Exile."
3 "Andrii Bogdanovich Za Artema Strizhakova!"

CHAPTER TEN – COMPLAIN TO THE BITTER END

1 Hrechka, "Iaki Problemy Na Vyborakh."
2 Law of Ukraine on Local Elections, 25.
3 Persha elektronna hazeta, "Cherez sumnivne rishennia."
4 Lystiuk, "Kirovohrads'ka Mis'ka TVK."
5 Lebid, "U Kirovohradi Ofitsiino Oholosyly Rezul'taty Vyboriv Mis'koho Holovy."
6 Ibid.

CHAPTER ELEVEN – CONCLUSIONS

1 Bjornlund, *Beyond Free and Fair*, 145.
2 Kelley, *Monitoring Democracy*, 61–2.
3 Kelley, "Election Observers and Their Biases."
4 Razumkov tsentr, "Pochatok Novoho Politychnoho Roku."
5 Transparency International, "2021 Corruption Perceptions Index."
6 Kelley, *Monitoring Democracy*, 167.
7 OSCE/ODIHR, "Ukraine Presidential Election 31 October, 21 November, and 26 December 2004," 1.
8 OSCE/ODIHR, "Republic of Tajikistan," 1.
9 OSCE/ODIHR, "Republic of Kazakhstan," 1.

10 Wołowska, "The OSCE Chairmanship."
11 Simpser and Donno, "Can International Election Monitoring Harm Governance?"
12 Hyde, *The Pseudo-Democrat's Dilemma*, 181.

EPILOGUE

1 OSCE/ODIHR, "Ukraine Presidential Election 31 March and 21 April 2019."
2 Bez Kupiur, "TSVK zatverdyla sklad."
3 Kolomoïtsev, "Ėks-Regional Strizhakov Protiv Raĭkovicha."
4 Hirsh, "2022."
5 Transparency International, "Ukraine."

Bibliography

"2020 Belarussian Presidential Election." Wikipedia, last edited 3 December
    2022. https://en.wikipedia.org/w/index.php?title=2020_Belarusian_
    presidential_election.

"Andriĭ Bogdanovich Za Artema Strizhakova!" Artem Strizhakov YouTube
    Channel, 15 October 2015. https://www.youtube.com/watch?v=OqV7_NFsgNA.

Association of Municipalities of Ontario. "Ontario Municipal Elections." Ontario
    Municipal Elections, 2022. https://elections2022.amo.on.ca/web/en/home.

Balmforth, Richard. "For Sale on Internet – Ukraine's Election Votes." Reuters,
    12 January 2010. https://www.reuters.com/article/ukraine-election-inter-
    net-idUSLDE60B0N020100112.

Bez Kupiŭr. "TSVK zatverdyla sklad okruzhnoï vyborchoï komisiï
    u Kropyvnytskomu." Bez Kupiŭr - Novyny Kropyvnyts'koho i
    Kirovohradshchyny, 11 April 2019. https://www.kypur.net/tsvk
    -zatverdyla-sklad-okruzhnoyi-vyborchoyi-komisiyi-u-kropyvnytskomu.

Bjornlund, Eric. *Beyond Free and Fair: Monitoring Elections and Building
    Democracy.* Washington, DC: Woodrow Wilson Center Press, 2004.

Boese, Vanessa A., Nazifa Alizada, Martin Lundstedt, Kelly Morrison, Natalia
    Natsika, Yuko Sato, Hugo Tai, and Staffan I. Lindberg. "Democracy Report
    2022: Autocratization Changing Nature?" *Varieties of Democracy Institute
    (V-Dem)*, 2022.

CANADEM. "Democracy Promotion and Election Observation." CANADEM, 2022.
    https://www.canadem.ca/democracy-elections.

CBC News. "All Prisoners Have the Right to Vote in the Federal Election.
    Here's How." 21 September 2019. https://www.cbc.ca/news/politics/
    canada-votes-2019-voting-incarcerated-house-arrest-1.5285711.

– "Elections Canada Working with Local Charities to Reduce Voting Barriers
    for People Who Are Homeless." 19 October 2019. https://www.cbc.ca/news/
    canada/kitchener-waterloo/homeless-voting-elections-canada-1.5325900.

Central Election Commission. "TSentralna Vyborcha Komisiia Ukraïny –
    www Vidobrazhennia IAS 'Vybory Narodnykh Deputativ Ukraïny 2014.'"
    31 October 2014. Accessed through archive.org. http://web.archive.org/

web/20141031113051/http://www.cvk.gov.ua/pls/vnd2014/wp040pt001f01=
910pf7331=99.html.

Chesno. "Tymoshenko I͡Uri͡ĭ Volodymyrovych." PolitHub, 2022.
https://www.chesno.org/politician/22705.

CIDA. "Evaluation of CIDA's Ukraine Program, 2004–2009." Ottawa: Canadian
International Development Agency, 2011.

Collins, Stephen. "Ireland's Voting System: How Does It Work and How Should I
Use It?" *The Irish Times*, 7 February 2020. https://www.irishtimes.com/news/
politics/ireland-s-voting-system-how-does-it-work-and-how-should-i
-use-it-1.4165178.

Depo.Kirovohrad. "U Stryz͡hakova Zai͡avyly, Shcho Naspravdi T͡se Vin Stav
Merom Kirovohrada – Novyny Kropyvnyt͡s'koho." Depo.ua, 15 November
2015. https://kr.depo.ua/ukr/kr/u-strizhakova-zayavili-shcho-naspravdi
-tse-vin-stav-merom-kirovograda-15112015234600.

Didenko, Andriy. "'Ukrainian Guantanamo' That Doesn't Exist. De Jure."
Kharkiv Human Rights Protection Group, 14 October 2011. https://khpg.
org//en/1318625800.

Dubyna, Svitlana. "Staly Vidomi Poperedni Rezul'taty Vyboriv Mis'koho
Holovy Kirovohrada u II Turi (ONOVLENO)." Hrechka – informat͡sii͡nyĭ
portal kirovohradshchyny, 16 November 2015. https://gre4ka.info/
suspilstvo/22469-vyborchi-komisii-oholosyly-rezultaty-vyboriv
-miskoho-holovy-kirovohrada-u-ii-turi.

Ferguson, Rob. "Ford Government Offers Ontario Nurses a $5K 'Retention'
Bonus." *Toronto Star*, 7 March 2022. https://www.thestar.com/politics/
provincial/2022/03/07/ford-government-offers-ontario-nurses-a-5k
-retention-bonus.html.

Fukuyama, Francis. "More Proof That This Really Is the End of History."
The Atlantic, 17 October 2022. https://www.theatlantic.com/ideas/
archive/2022/10/francis-fukuyama-still-end-history/671761.

Gee, Marcus. "Doug Ford Sent Me a $440 Licence Plate Renewal Refund,
but I Wish He Hadn't." *The Globe and Mail*, 6 April 2022. https://www.
theglobeandmail.com/canada/toronto/article-ford-license-plate-renewal
-refund-election-votes.

Global Affairs Canada. "Canada's Engagement in Ukraine." 22 March 2022.
https://www.international.gc.ca/country-pays/ukraine/relations.aspx.

– "Evaluation of the Stabilization and Reconstruction Task Force (START)
and Global Peace and Security Fund (GPSF)." 6 March 2018. https://www.
international.gc.ca/gac-amc/publications/evaluation/2018/start-gpsf.aspx.

Golosnoy, Maxim. "Who Is Maxim Golosnoy?" Accessed 26 January 2024.
https://golosnoy.com/en/who-is-maxim-golosnoy.

Hirsh, Michael. "2022: The Year the Good Guys Struck Back." *Foreign Policy*, 19 December 2022. https://foreignpolicy.com/2022/12/19/russia-ukraine-war-democracy-2022-authoritarianism-xenophobia.

Hrechka – informatsiĭnyĭ portal kirovohradshchyny. "ĬAki Problemy Na Vyborakh Zafiksuvaly Kandydaty Na Posadu Mera Kirovohrada?" 15 November 2015. https://gre4ka.info/suspilstvo/22457-yaki-problemy-na-vyborakh-zafiksuvaly-kandydaty-na-posadu-mera-kirovohrada.

Hudson Institute. "Ukraine's Rectification of Names." 23 June 2016. http://www.hudson.org/research/12590-ukraine-s-rectification-of-names.

Hyde, Susan D. *The Pseudo-Democrat's Dilemma: Why Election Observation Became an International Norm.* Cornell, NY: Cornell University Press, 2011.

IOM. "IOM's Assistant to Internally Displaced Persons in Ukraine, November 2015." International Organization for Migration, November 2015. https://www.iom.int/sites/g/files/tmzbdl486/files/situation_reports/file/IOM-Ukraine-IDP-Assistance-Report-November-2015.pdf.

Käihkö, Ilmari. "A Nation-in-the-Making, in Arms: Control of Force, Strategy and the Ukrainian Volunteer Battalions." *Defence Studies* 18, no. 2 (3 April 2018): 147–66. https://doi.org/10.1080/14702436.2018.1461013.

Kelley, Judith. "Election Observers and Their Biases." *Journal of Democracy* 21, no. 3 (2010). https://www.journalofdemocracy.org/articles/election-observers-and-their-biases.

Kelley, Judith G. *Monitoring Democracy.* Princeton, NJ: Princeton University Press, 2012.

Kolomoĭtsev, Anton. "Ėks-Regional Strizhakov Protiv Raĭkovicha: Glavnye Intrigi Mestnykh Vyborov v Kropivnitskom." Depo.ua, 24 September 2020. https://www.depo.ua/rus/politics/mistsevi-vibori-v-kropivnitskomu-chomu-raykovich-strimko-zrostae-u-reytingakh-202009231219359.

Law of Ukraine on Local Elections. OSCE/ODIHR Translation. 2015.

Lebid, Valeriĭ. "U Kirovohradi Ofitsiĭno Oholosyly Rezultaty Vyboriv Miskoho Holovy (FOTO)." Hrechka – informatsiĭnyĭ portal kirovohradshchyny, 23 November 2015. https://gre4ka.info/polityka/22607-u-kirovohradi-ofitsiino-oholosyly-rezultaty-vyboriv-miskoho-holovy-foto.

Likhachev, Vyacheslav. "The 'Right Sector' and Others: The Behavior and Role of Radical Nationalists in the Ukrainian Political Crisis of Late 2013 – Early 2014." *Communist and Post-Communist Studies* 48, nos. 2/3 (2015): 257–71.

Lystiŭk, Svitlana. "Kirovohradska Miska TVK Hotuĭetsia Zrobyty Raĭkovycha Miskym Holovoiu." Persha elektronna hazeta, 21 November 2015. https://persha.kr.ua/news/politics/59500-kirovogradska-miska-tvk-gotuyetsya-zrobiti-rajkovicha-miskim-golovoyu.

Opening Doors. "100,000 Children in Ukraine Confined to Soviet-Style Orphanage System That Resists Reform." 2017. https://www.openingdoors. eu/100000-children-in-ukraine-confined-to-soviet-style-orphanage-system -that-resists-reform.

OSCE/ODIHR. *Handbook for Long-Term Election Observers: Beyond Election Day Observation.* Warsaw: OSCE/ODIHR, 2007.

– "Republic of Belarus Presidential Election 19 December 2010: OSCE/ODIHR Election Observation Mission Final Report." Warsaw: OSCE/ODIHR, 2011.

– "Republic of Kazakhstan Parliamentary Elections, 18 August 2007: OSCE/ODIHR Election Observation Mission Report." Warsaw: OSCE/ODIHR, 2007.

– "Republic of Tajikistan Presidential Election, 6 November 2006: OSCE/ODIHR Election Observation Mission Report." Warsaw: OSCE/ODIHR, 2007.

– "Ukraine Early Parliamentary Elections 26 October 2014: OSCE/ODIHR Election Observation Mission Final Report." Warsaw: OSCE/ODIHR, 2014.

– "Ukraine Early Presidential Elections 25 May 2014: OSCE/ODIHR Election Observation Mission Final Report." Warsaw: OSCE/ODIHR, 2014.

– "Ukraine Local Elections 25 October and 15 November 2015: OSCE/ODIHR Election Observation Mission Final Report." Warsaw: OSCE/ODIHR, 2016.

– "Ukraine Parliamentary Elections 28 October 2012: ODIHR Election Observation Mission Final Report." Washington: OSCE/ODIHR, 2013.

– "Ukraine Presidential Election 31 March and 21 April 2019 ODIHR Election Observation Mission Final Report." Warsaw: OSCE/ODIHR, 2019.

– "Ukraine Presidential Election 31 October, 21 November, and 26 December 2004: OSCE/ODIHR Election Observation Mission Final Report." Warsaw: OSCE/ODIHR, 2005.

Persha elektronna hazeta. "Cherez sumnivne rishennia miskvyborchkomu stavsia skandal na zasidanni DVK №350867 (FOTO, VIDEO)." 22 November 2015. https://persha.kr.ua/news/politics/59550-cherez-sumnivne-rishennya -miskviborchkomu-stavsya-skandal-na-zasidanni-dvk-350867-foto-video.

Razumkov tsentr. "Pochatok Novoho Politychnoho Roku: Dovira Do Sotsialnykh Instytutiv (Lypen 2020r.)." 4 September 2020. https://razumkov. org.ua/napriamky/sotsiologichni-doslidzhennia/pochatok-novogo -politychnogo-roku-dovira-do-sotsialnykh-instytutiv-lypen-2020r.

ReliefWeb. "Ukraine IDP Figures Analysis (as of October 2014)." 31 October 2014. https://reliefweb.int/report/ukraine/ukraine-idp-figures-analysis-october-2014.

Repucci, Sarah, and Amy Slipowitz. "Freedom in the World 2022: The Global Expansion of Authoritarian Rule." Washington, DC: Freedom House, 2022. https://freedomhouse.org/sites/default/files/2022-02/FIW_2022_PDF_ Booklet_Digital_Final_Web.pdf.

Romaniuk, Anatole, and Oleksandr Gladun. "Demographic Trends in Ukraine: Past, Present, and Future." *Population and Development Review* 41, no. 2 (2015): 315–37.

Scrutton, Alistair, and Seema Shah, eds. *The Global State of Democracy 2022: Forging Social Contracts in a Time of Discontent*. Global State of Democracy Initiative. Stockholm: International Institute for Democracy and Electoral Assistance, 2022. https://doi.org/10.31752/idea.2022.56.

Shevel, Oxana. "The Repeat Second Round of the 2004 Presidential Elections in Kirovohrad." In Aspects of the Orange Revolution IV – *Foreign Assistance and Civic Action in the 2004 Ukrainian Presidential Elections: Soviet and Post-Soviet Politics and Society*. Boston, MA: Tufts University, 2007. https://wikis.uit.tufts.edu/confluence/download/attachments/23235422/2007_OrangeRevIVKirovohrad.pdf.

Simpser, Alberto, and Daniela Donno. "Can International Election Monitoring Harm Governance?" *The Journal of Politics* 74, no. 2 (2012): 501–13.

Snyder, Timothy. *Bloodlands: Europe between Hitler and Stalin*. New York: Basic Books (AZ), 2010.

Statistics Canada. "Census in Brief: Ethnic and Cultural Origins of Canadians: Portrait of a Rich Heritage." 25 October 2017. https://www12.statcan.gc.ca/census-recensement/2016/as-sa/98-200-x/2016016/98-200-x2016016-eng.cfm.

– "Voter Turnout Rates by Age Group, Province and Immigrant Status, 2011, 2015, 2019 and 2021 Federal Elections." 16 February 2022. https://www150.statcan.gc.ca/n1/daily-quotidien/220216/t001d-eng.htm.

Szostek, Joanna. "Nothing Is True? The Credibility of News and Conflicting Narratives during 'Information War' in Ukraine." *The International Journal of Press/Politics* 23, no. 1 (1 January 2018): 116–35. https://doi.org/10.1177/1940161217743258.

Talant, Bermet. "Savik Shuster Returns as TV Host after Exile." *Kyiv Post*, 13 September 2019. https://www.kyivpost.com/ukraine-politics/savik-shuster-returns-as-tv-host-after-exile.html.

Transparency International. "2021 Corruption Perceptions Index – Explore the Results," 2022. https://www.transparency.org/en/cpi/2021.

– "Ukraine – Corruptions Perceptions Index," 2021. https://www.transparency.org/en/countries/ukraine.

Trebunsky, Irina. "Vyborchi Komisiï Na Kirovohradshchyni: Khto Platytʹ Ta Khto Holovuie?" *Narodni Slova*, 19 August 2020. https://n-slovo.com.ua/2020/08/19/виборчі-комісії-на-кіровоградщині-хт/.

Trishyna, Nataliia. "Vidterminovanyĭ Revansh: Stryzhakov Vdruhe Balotuvatymetsia Na Posadu Miskoho Holovy." Suspilne Novyny, 17 September 2020. https://suspilne.media/63743-vidterminovanij-revans-strizakov-vdruge-balotuvatimetsa-na-posadu-miskogo-golovi.

Uggen, Christopher. "Locked Out 2020: Estimates of People Denied Voting Rights Due to a Felony Conviction." Washington, DC: The Sentencing Project, 2020. https://www.sentencingproject.org/publications/locked-out-2020 -estimates-of-people-denied-voting-rights-due-to-a-felony-conviction.

"Vecherniĭ Kvartal Ot 19.10.2012." Studiâ Kvartal 95 Online YouTube channel. 2012, uploaded 16 September 2013. https://www.youtube.com/watch?v=_byogBNMU1I.

Williams, Phil, and John Picarelli. "Organized Crime in Ukraine: Challenge and Response." Washington, DC: US Department of Justice, 2002.

Wołowska, Anna. "The OSCE Chairmanship – Kazakhstan's Self-Promotion Campaign?" OSW Commentary. Centre for Eastern Studies, 2010.

Woodward, Bob, and Carl Bernstein. *All the President's Men*. Simon and Schuster, 2014.

Worldometer. "Ukraine Population (2022)." 2022. https://www.worldometers. info/world-population/ukraine-population.

Yakovenko, Iryna, Oleksandra Poloskova, Yevhen Solonyna, and Daisy Sindelar. "A Sticky Situation for Poroshenko as Russians Seize Candy Assets." *Radio Free Europe/Radio Liberty*, 29 April 2015. https://www.rferl.org/a/ukraine -poroshenko-roshen-russia-seizes-candy-lipetsk/26985196.html.

Index